1.00

HANDBOOK OF CANARIES

DR. MATTHEW M. VRIENDS

Photography:
Black and White: by Dr. Herbert R. Axelrod, Harry V. Lacey and Louise van der Meid.

Color: Harry V. Lacey: 68, 69, 72, 73, 76, 77, 80, 84, 85, 88, 89, 92, 93, 193, 196, 197, 200, 201, 204, 205, 208, 209, 212, 213, 216, 217, 220, 221, 224, 289, 292; Vogelpark Walsrode: backcover, 65, 293, 300, 301, 304, 305, 308, 309, 312, 313, 316, 317, 320; Dr. Matthew M. Vriends: 296, 297.

Frontis: Green Border Fancy canary.

ISBN 0-87666-876-7

© 1980 by T.F.H. Publications, Inc. Ltd.

Distributed in the U.S. by T.F.H. Publications, Inc., 211 West Sylvania Avenue, PO Box 427, Neptune, NJ 07753; in England by T.F.H. (Gt. Britain) Ltd., 13 Nutley Lane, Reigate, Surrey; in Canada to the book store and library trade by Beaverbooks Ltd., 150 Lesmill Road, Don Mills, Ontario M38 2T5, Canada; in Canada to the pet trade by Rolf C. Hagen Ltd., 3225 Sartelon Street, Montreal 382, Quebec; in Southeast Asia by Y.W. Ong, 9 Lorong 36 Geylang, Singapore 14; in Australia and the South Pacific by Pet Imports Pty. Ltd., P.O. Box 149, Brookvale 2100, N.S.W. Australia; in South Africa by Valid Agencies, P.O. Box 51901, Randburg 2125 South Africa. Published by T.F.H. Publications, Inc., Ltd, the British Crown Colony of Hong Kong.

Contents

INTRODUCTION................................ 7
1. A LITTLE HISTORY........................ 17
2. HOUSING CANARIES IN CAGES
   AND AVIARIES............................. 37
   Cages, 40; The location, 44; The box cage, 47; Sand on the cage bottom, 47; Covering the cage, 48; Caution is the watchword, 49; Keeping the cage clean, 52; Baths, 52; Fancy clothespins, 55; Care during the summer months, 56; What do our canaries require from us?, 56; Canaries in a community aviary, 59; Aviaries, 63; Location, 66; Material, 66; Shape and size, 70; Layout, 70; The open area, 74; The covered area, 78; The closed area, 78; General remarks, 82; Bird room, 82; Indoor aviary, 87; Shrubbery, 90; Maintenance, 103.
3. CARE AND FEEDING OF THE CANARY........107
   Water, 123; Coprophagy, 127; Seeds, 128; Weeds, 130; Sprouted seed, 142; Chick rearing and strength foods, 143; Greens, 146; Fruit, 146; Minerals, 147; Grit and cuttlebone, 147; Lard, 147.
4. A LITTLE ORNITHOLOGY....................149
   General trademarks, 150; Feathers, 151; Flying, 153; Propulsion, 154; Respiration, 158.
5. KEEPING CANARIES........................161
   What does a good canary look like?, 161; The selection, 163; Which canaries do we choose? 166; Breeding the citron canary, 168; Requirements for color canaries, 172; Washing birds, 175; Top condition, 178.
6. DISEASE, ACCIDENTS, AND PARASITES......181
   Diarrhea or intestinal catarrh, 182; Constipation, 187; Gout and/or rheumatism, 187; Colds, 189; Tumors, 191; Fractures, 191; Balance problems, 198; Hoarseness, 198; Baldness and molting, 199; Sore or infected eyes, 202; Sickle nails, 203; Calcified feet, 203; Infected oil gland, 203; Egg binding, 206; Fatty degeneration, 207; Constant over-eating, 210; Feather plucking, 211; Egg pecking, 214; Parasites, 215; Cholera, 215; Tuberculosis, 218; Smallpox and diphtheria, 218; Canary pox, 218; Sweating sickness, 225; Fast and painless killing of canaries, 225.

7. BREEDING CANARIES.......................229
   The miracle of chromosomes, 229; Recessive and dominant factors, 240; Sex-linked heredity, 241; Genes, 244; Lethal factor, 245; Pairing, 245; Nests, 248; Manner of breeding, 252; Alternate breeding method, 252; Feeding canaries during the breeding season, 258; The ringing of canaries, 260; The chicks, 260.
8. COLOR CANARIES...........................263
   Yellow canaries, 264; Citron, 265; White canaries, 268; Color canary varieties, 269; Brown canaries, 272; Once again: sex-linked inheritance, 274; Heredity of brown, 276; Brown and citron brown, 277; Gold brown canaries, 277; Intensive and frosted (non-intensive), 278; Green canaries, 280; The silver brown canary, 281; The blue canaries, 282; Agate and isabel, 283; Agates that lack the red factor, 285; Isabels that lack the red factor, 286; The popular red factor, 290; Red orange bronze and frosted red orange bronze (= non-intensive), 290; Red bronze and frosted red bronze, 290; Orange brown and frosted orange brown, 290; Red orange brown and frosted red orange brown, 291; Orange agate and frosted orange agate, 291; Red orange agate and frosted red orange agate, 294; Red agate and frosted red agate, 294; Orange isabel and frosted orange isabel, 294; Red orange isabel and frosted red orange isabel, 295; Red isabel and frosted red isabel, 298; Lipochrome and the red factor, 298; Apricot, 298; Intensive orange, 299; Red orange intensive, 299; Red, 299; Dimorphic canaries, 299; Pigmented dimorphic, 302; The pastel factor, 302; The ivory factor, 306; The opal factor, 307; The inos, 307; Possible crosses with wild songbirds, 307.
9. FORM AND POSTURE CANARIES.............311
   The Belgian Bult, 314; Crested canary, 319; The Yorkshire, 318; Scotch Fancy, 323; Norwich canary, 324; Border canary, 326; Gloster Corona, 328; Lizard canary, 330; Parisian Frill, 332; Gibber Italicus or Italian Humpback Frill, 334, Northern Dutch Frill, 335; Southern Dutch Frill, 338; Bernese canary, 339; Final notes, 342.
   BIBLIOGRAPHY
   ILLUSTRATIONS INDEX

"Soyons fidèles à nos faiblesses"

In memory of my father C. Vriends
an excellent birdman and teacher
and a good friend.

Female Border canary at her nest with chicks.

INTRODUCTION

It is probably common knowledge to the average reader that the male canary has an excellent reputation as a singer, but of course, any one male could be a better singer than the next. In breeders' circles one generally speaks of Harz canaries when referring to really good singers. These birds are descendants of the wild canary (*Serinus canarius*) which is found, among other places, in the Canary Islands and was brought to Europe some four and a half centuries ago by Portuguese sailors.

The wild canary is a greyish green bird, but through breeding skills and spontaneous color changes which we call "mutations," the green pied, yellow pied, and even a clear yellow canary were developed in the Harz Mountains, where the Harz canary got its name. The song of the Harz birds (which, incidentally, can be purchased in any good pet store) has very little left in common with that of the wild canary. Through strict selection and a never-ending search for birds with certain song "tours," a canary song repertoire has been established which is soft, melodious and has many variations. A Harz breeder is not at all concerned with coloring, and experience has shown that birds with the least attractive plumage—the green pied variety—have the most beautiful voices and claim the highest prizes at shows!

The color breeder, of course, sets different standards. He is not concerned with song but only with color and continuously searches for new ways which will enable him to improve the coloring of his birds. It will, no doubt, not be earth-shattering news to most readers that there are red,

The Hooded Siskin, a tropical bird crossed with the canary to produce red factor coloring.

orange, dark brown, lemon yellow, light brown, white, blue, silver, and gold canaries. This represents only a small part of the rich variety in colors and shades, not to mention the several combinations that are possible from all these colors. As an example, the red orange agate and the red orange isabel are very popular; red orange agate is red with dark brown, and red orange isabel is red with light brown and beige.

Some of these colors came into existence through the crossing of the canary with a tropical bird, the hooded siskin (*Spinus cucullata*). This bird is primarily red with a black head, and, though he is somewhat smaller than the canary, the male of this species is currently one of the few birds that can be crossed with the canary hen. Happily the males of the resulting offspring are, for the most part, fertile. These hybrids inherit the red from their father and are then crossed back with canaries. After the fourth generation, the birds are again identical to canaries, as if their ancestors were all true canaries. In the beginning stages of these breeding experiments, which took place around the turn of the century in Lochem (Holland) and surrounding areas, the only canaries available were yellow Harz hens, with the result that the offspring were a very vague, dull orange. But after a few years the hens kept inheriting stronger colors, because the best orange birds were continuously selected to be cross-bred with the hooded siskin.

Before World War II there were practically no birds that even suggested a deep red. Most were orange canaries, and it was a mystery as to why the red of the siskin could not be achieved. Through sheer coincidence it was discovered, however, that certain foodstuffs appear to have an influence at least on the orange color. If foods containing a carotenoid substance were given, the orange color became considerably stronger. Carotenoid can be found in various vegetables and in considerable amounts in carrots and kale. Owners of orange or red canaries are advised to hang a fresh

Lancashire Coppy canary, a very old English breed which has recently been "bred back" from near extinction.

carrot in the cage or aviary every day in a location where the birds can nibble at it comfortably. There is nothing unsporting about this from a breeder's point of view. To maintain their beautiful color, red factor canaries simply need certain substances which cannot be found in a package of canary seed or the traditional sprout or leaf of lettuce, which often constitutes their diet. But even when carrots are added to the diet, a bird's color cannot be changed to deep red; at best it becomes a deep orange. To achieve red, stronger substances must come into play, namely preparations which have cayenne pepper as the main ingredient. Whether these preparations should be administered or not causes some controversy in breeders' circles. However, as

The Lizard canary, capped and with a series of black crescent-shaped spots running in orderly parallel rows down the back of the bird in a spangling effect produced by the overlapping of the saddle feathers.

long as a true red canary is not produced through natural means, these preparations will, no doubt, still be used quite a lot.

Individuals who purchase a red canary in a bird shop for a considerable sum often come to the unhappy conclusion after the first molt that their red pet has turned orange. If no color foods and not even carrots have been given during the molting period, this change of color is perfectly normal. The red color was not natural but was brought about through artificial means, so one need not worry that there is something amiss with the bird. If your bird starts to sing again in his usual lusty manner after the molting period is over, this is a sign that all is well. Color canaries also sing, of course, but their song is remarkably different from that of Harz canaries. Along with the color from the hooded

A good Border male except for the fact that he is too large and sits with a bulge in his back.

Green Border Fancy canary. Border breeders prefer a bird that most closely approximates grass green.

siskin, the canary also inherited certain voice characteristics. A healthy canary will sing as lustily as a Harz, but his song is much louder. Yet it is noteworthy that most people who have just one canary in a cage kept in their living room or kitchen prefer one that sings loudly. In addition, the clear yellow canary is still the favorite color, but the color canary fancy is a special hobby which attracts tens of thousands of enthusiasts. Most are members of a club, and many of these clubs get together once a year to conduct competitions and exhibitions.

New colors and new cross-breeding possibilities are still sought in which the offspring will prove to be fertile. The goal of every color canary breeder is to come up with a sky blue or a black canary, but the first blue has a very poor chance. Time and time again, efforts have been made to this end by crossing with blue partners such as the indigo finch, but these two birds are barely related, and one would have to be quite an optimist to place them together! The situation is a little different with better chances for

Yorkshire canary of the self-green variety. Through strict selection the canary song repertoire which has been established greatly differs from that of the wild canary.

breeding a black canary. Both the original wild canary as well as the hooded siskin have black pigmentation in their plumage, and there is always the possibility that a completely black mutant will some day appear. The yellow canary was started this way, so there is no reason why a black mutant could not appear.

In any event, I will speak more on this subject and many others in this book and have decided to start with the practical aspects. You will not come across any particularly difficult theory, and the same holds true in the chapter covering genetics. There are several good books available on canaries and everything to do with them, so those who wish to delve into the genetics of these birds more deeply will have no problems in finding appropriate literature. This book has been written for those fanciers who would like to keep and breed canaries in a responsible manner, and it is not really necessary to acquire more books, although we can never know too much about the birds entrusted to our care!

I would like to thank Mrs. T. Williams-Parent for her fine translations and editing. On top of this, she has uncomplainingly typed the manuscript. Mr. Remi Ceuleers is thanked for his suggestions and for making available the literature I requested. Once again, I would like to thank my wife, Lucy Vriends-Parent, for her constant encouragement and enthusiasm as well as her spontaneous cooperation in the writing of this book. Without her this work could never have been realized. Any suggestions that would improve or complete this book are, as always, sincerely welcome so they may be included in any further editions.

Dr. Matthew M. Vriends

Neptune, New Jersey

Border Fancy canary (left) and Gloster Fancy canary (right). When we consider the current rich variety of colors we see that the canary has come a long way from its ancestor in the wild.

1: A LITTLE HISTORY

When we take a look at the world of birds, with its 8,600-odd different species, it might be considered remarkable that the wild canary, an anything but striking little bird, has developed in a matter of a few hundred years to the point where absolutely everyone is familiar with it. Even the most ignorant in the field of biology can recognize and identify the canary. This little bird (*Serinus canarius* or *Fringilla canaria*) has drastically changed if we consider the rich variety of colors, of which the first canary breeders would not have dared even dream. Presently related canaries of a different species (European canary) can be found throughout most of Europe and even in parts of Asia. Of course ornithologists—the professional bird scientists—have divided canaries into various groups, but the most important one for the aviculturist (the cage and aviary hobbyist) is obviously the one that lives in the Canary Islands and on Madeira. This wild canary is olive green in color with a number of greyish brown stripes, which are yellow in the males though not very obvious and certainly not a basis for comparison with the yellow of our current yellow canaries. No matter how dark or ordinary looking the wild canary may be, he is still the ancestor of our current song, color, and posture canaries . . . quite an honor to say the least!

There are several stories claiming to tell of the "discovery" of the wild canary. It is alleged, for example, that a French sailor married a native girl in the Canary Islands and then discovered the wild canary. The Canary Islands, incidentally, are located in the Atlantic Ocean off the western coast of Africa and consist of Hierro, Palma,

Gomera, Teneriffe, Grand Canaria, Fuerteventura, Lanzarote, Graciosa, Alegranza, Sante Clara, Lobes, and Rorca. The sailor's name was Jean de Bethancourt. Although he lived mostly from farming and fishing, he built small cages in his spare time, filled them with canaries, and shipped them to Spain on vessels sailing under the Spanish flag. Thus Spain would have received the first canaries. We will have to accept this story for what it is worth; it really is not all that important whether we believe it or not. What is certain, however, is that in the sixteenth and seventeenth centuries canaries were already being bred in several places. In the fifteenth century they are alleged to have already been bred on quite a large scale in Spain.

There is also a story which states that during the fifteenth century the Spanish held a very tight rein on the canary market and exported just a few males to Italy and Switzerland. In one of these exports, however, a mistake seems to have been made and a female ended up in the hands of a priest, who started to breed her. It is very likely that this female was mistaken for a male because of her coloring, or perhaps her song was a lot like that of the male. Here again, we will reserve judgment with regard to the validity of the story.

The most well-known story is that of a Spanish ship that was surprised by a storm on the coast of Italy on its way to Livorno. No doubt there were sailors who felt sorry for the cargo—which consisted of canaries—and in their compassion freed them. In any event, canaries were found on Elba for a considerable period of time. From Elba they would have come to the mainland. The fact remains that now, however, canaries are no longer to be found on Elba.

Be sure not to confuse the wild canary, ancestor of our domestic canaries, with the European canary; ornithologically, we are dealing here with two different species. In other words, the European canary can still be found on Elba, but not the wild canary. It is, therefore, best to no

Gloster Fancy canary (left) and Border Fancy canary (right). The wild canary is the ancestor of our current song, color, and posture canaries.

longer speak in this book of the European canary and the wild canary. It is little wonder that most canary fanciers incorrectly think of a single bird when they speak of the wild canary and the European canary, because most canary books use the two names interchangeably.

In any event, canaries would have come to Elba because of the sinking of the Spanish vessel. The birds would have flown westwards and landed on Elba, where the ideal weather conditions favored the subsequent enlargement of their families! The Italians, who have been known for centuries as the number-one bird catchers of the world, no doubt saw money in these lusty little singers, caught them by the thousands, and brought them to the mainland. From there they were taken to northern Italy, to the Tyrol, and to areas in Germany. In Germany, where bird and canary

Green Border Fancy canaries. There is a large variety of coloration in the green series.

clubs were established toward the end of the eighteenth century, they were successfully bred and marketed. It was not long before there were also canary fanciers in England and Russia. The prices were not very high, it would seem, because the best breeders were to be found among the working class. We should also mention the poor mountain folk of the Harz area (Germany), who bred canaries not only as a good supplemental income, but also because they had a great love for these small birds. This is not to imply that the peddlers sold their birds for low prices. Stork (*Kanaries*) says in this regard:

"In our Low Countries (Holland), canaries were imported from Germany and Belgium particularly in the nineteenth and in the beginning of the twentieth centuries. The Netherlands already had some canary breeders herself, but apparently there was such a demand for canaries that the foreign peddlers had no trouble selling their birds. These peddlers were a common sight in our towns and villages at that time. They carried on their backs a wooden rack which had a great many little cages attached to it, with four to six canaries in each cage. The whole contraption was tied to the back of the peddler with belts and was covered with a canvas, which was rolled up in good weather. The peddler could be heard coming from quite a distance, because the birds had grown accustomed to their nomadic existence and sang to their hearts' content.

"These peddlers traveled from town to town and from village to village. They usually spent a few days in a particular lodging, awaiting buyers who were made aware of

Pigmented yellow canary. The basic yellow coloring of the canary, lipochrome, is derived from carotenoid substances in the bird's diet.

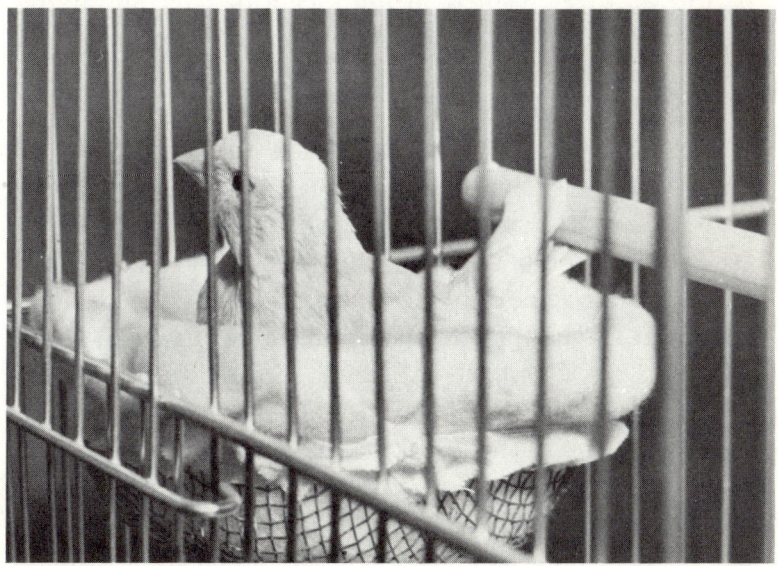

Pigmented yellow canary. The actual shade of coloring can vary considerably and is controlled by sex, heredity, and feeding.

the peddler's visit by an advertisement placed in the local paper. With sales the cages became emptier, in contrast to the peddler's wallet; in the meantime, his supply of the niger seed with which he fed his canaries was also steadily being depleted. The peddlers usually bred their own birds. They lived in the Harz, the Black Forest, in Zwaben, and in Bavaria, as well as in the vicinity of Liege. As soon as the breeding season was over and the young birds had started to sing, the peddler buckled his rack to his back and started the peddling journey. This was quite an achievement, especially when we consider that these travelings often lasted until the spring and that the peddler walked the entire way. Many of them often went back to the same lodgings, and they were generally considered the most honest because one could then feel assured that the peddler could be located if something ailed the purchased bird. These peddlers acquired a fair use of the Dutch language, and they must have made a very decent living, because good singers could procure as much as twenty guilders and more, and that in a time when a working man seldom earned more than ten guilders a week!"

England, too, used Harz canaries, but this country, which had always had an important place in avicultural matters, soon determined her own route and did a great job in perfecting song canaries within her own borders. This, of course, was to be expected since the wild canary was "elevated" to song canary because of its singing talents, although this work should not be underestimated. In decadent France, men used musical instruments to enrich the canary's song; in fact, even special little flutes were made as described in the book written by Hervieux de Chanteloup,

The Yorkshire canary is derived from crosses involving the Lancashire Plainhead, Norwich (old-fashioned type), and the Belgian.

Norwich canary. The feathering of the Norwich is short and compact with the polished sheen of silk.

who was connected with the Court of King Louis XIV. It is certainly interesting that this man even tried to teach the canary to imitate the human voice, though, of course, he never succeeded! We currently know that crows and the well-known hook-beaked birds—the parrots and parrakeets—are capable of imitating the human voice. Starlings also possess this ability, as well as the ability to imitate the song of other birds, so when listening to the starling it is quite possible to hear the songs of four or five different bird species. Chanteloup's book also speaks of color canaries and gives us a good insight into the knowledge available to man at that time on song and color canaries. Chanteloup, who became mentally imbalanced later in his life, entitled his book *Nouveau Traite des Serins de Canarie* and listed the following colors:

1. Serin gris commun, i.e., the ordinary self green canary.
2. Serin gris aux duvets et aux pattes blanches, i.e. self green canary with white underfeathering and feet.
3. Serin gris a queue blanche, i.e. self green canary with white tail.
4. Serin blond commun, i.e. agate (or dilute) canary.
5. Serin blond aux yeux rouges, i.e. agate canary with pink eyes.
6. Serin jaune commun, i.e. common yellow canary.
7. Serin jaune aux duvets, i.e. common yellow canary with white underfeathering.
8. Serin jaune a queue blanche, i.e. common yellow canary with white tail.

This book, that was first published in 1713, had several later editions. In a Dutch translation dating from 1717, just four years after the original version, the color varieties already numbered 28, as follows:

1. Common self green.
2. Self green with white underfeathering and feet.
3. Self green with white tail.
4. Ash-grey.
5. Ash-grey with pink eyes.
6. Golden-yellow ash-grey.
7. Ash-grey with wild-type plumage (downy variety).
8. Ash-grey, white-tailed, with wild-type plumage.
9. Downy yellow with wild plumage.
10. Common yellow.
11. Yellow, with white tail and wild-type plumage.
12. Common agate.

Two Parisian Frills display the principal kinds of frills from long, flowing fine plumes to shorter, crisper ones with tight curling.

13. Agate with pink eyes.
14. Agate with white tail and wild-type plumage.
15. Downy agate with wild-type plumage.
16. Common isabel.
17. Isabel with pink eyes.
18. Gold isabel.
19. Downy isabel with wild-type plumage.
20. Isabel with white tail and wild-type plumage.
21. White with pink eyes.
22. Common wild-type plumage.
23. Wild-type plumage with pink eyes.
24. Ash-grey with wild-type plumage.

25. Ash-grey with wild-type plumage and pink eyes.
26. Black with wild-type plumage.
27. Black and yellow with wild-type plumage and pink eyes.
28. Black with wild-type plumage and regular markings.

It is apparent from these rather strange sounding listings that quite a lot was already known about color canaries well over 200 years ago. Considering the number of times that pink eyes are mentioned, one might question exactly where this factor came from, and more importantly, where has it gone? One might assume these canaries were actually albinos or lutinos, which have red eyes. On the other hand, there are canary colors mentioned that are currently classified as the so-called pigmented canaries. If these did indeed have pink eyes, and there is no reason why this

The Corona is the crested type of Gloster Fancy canary.

Norwich canary, called "the John Bull of the canary world" for its rotund, stocky build.

could not have been possible, then it becomes clear that there is nothing so unusual with our current canaries. I would like to point out that the so-called ino canaries first appeared in 1964. If Hervieux was stating the truth in his book, then it is altogether possible that the present-day ino is the same mutation that our French bird fancier speaks of!

The Dutch author van Wickede wrote in 1750 (in his book *Kanarie uitspanningen of nieuwe verhandelingen van de Kanarieteelt*) on color varieties which are also currently well known and loved. I am thinking here of the agate and the isabel, feuille morte, white, and yellow; yes, even the albino seems to have existed . . . a bird that is no longer even among our canaries! It is, incidentally, interesting to follow

F. van Wickede in his writings about hybrids. The currently well-known crossbreedings between goldfinch, siskin, chaffinch, redpoll, greenfinch, etc., were already quite common in his time; in fact, even crossings between insect-eating birds such as the hedgesparrow and the wagtail were common! If what van Wickede says is indeed true, the bird fanciers and breeders at that time certainly deserve to take a bow. Where today could we find a crossing between a wagtail and a canary? And when I say where, I mean where in the entire world!

I imagine the reader has been able to ascertain from the preceding pages that quite a lot has happened to the wild canary since it was first discovered. The color, posture and especially the song have each undergone substantial development. While originally the nightingale was often placed as champion singer, it was soon discovered that, just as with our goldfinch, the wild canary was also capable and willing to imitate the song of other birds. The Germans were true masters in the development of the canary's song. I urge you, for interest's sake, to attend a singing competition or an exhibition where song canaries are being judged. You will be astounded by their repertoire of "rolls" and "tours" as they are called, such as the Hollow Roll, Bass Roll, Water Glucke, Schockel, and the Hollow Bell, to mention a few. The Harz or roller canary was developed for its song and is still much loved and often bred today. The posture canaries also started to draw more attention, and since every bird more or less had its own beginning, followed by an often very interesting history, I felt it wise to spend ample time on these somewhat strange creatures. From the notations made under this group, it will hopefully become clear that the posture canaries also capture quite a share of interest and wonder and by no means should be thought of as "unsuccessful products" of canary breeding.

Ornithologists have quite a lot of data gleaned from centuries-old books. Don't forget that the canary has

Green Border Fancy canary, a lightly built active bird.

"only" been domesticated for five centuries. In other words, thanks to the advent of printing, many interesting and sometimes incredible details have been acquired. Much of this information has since been superseded. Nevertheless, from reading these old, often very valuable texts, ornithologists do realize that even the breeders of long ago had a surprisingly good knowledge and background with regard to the care and breeding of these birds. In the middle of the 16th century, Konrad Gessner described the canary in his *Avium Nature* (*The Natural History of Birds*). Although he had never seen a canary himself, the details had been passed on to him by a few friends who were bird enthusiasts. Gessner calls the canary "Canaria Avicula," and, indeed, the canary was also long known as "cane" or "sugar cane" bird ("can(n)a" means (sugar) cane). Even today most fanciers are convinced that canaries are crazy about sugar . . . many a sugar cube and cookie has been offered through the bars and gratefully devoured. If we do not make a too frequent habit of this, it certainly will not do any harm!

Aldrovandi, an Italian scholar connected with the University of Bologna, wrote about the canary in one of his many papers and stated that the cock can be readily distinguished from the hen by his more intense yellow coloring; he also included an illustration, albeit a rather poor one! A very beautiful illustration, however, can be found in the book written by G. Olina and published in Rome in 1622; this illustration can be found repeatedly in later works. Toward the end of the nineteenth century, the experts in the field seemed to be, in particular, Dr. Karl Rusz in Germany and A. Nuyers and J.H. Beekman in the Netherlands. All three wrote interesting and instructive literature. There is currently no shortage in the selection of canary books available on the market.

The intensity of efforts made by the breeders in the Harz Mountains, and in St. Andreasberg in particular, is illustrated by Van der Mark in his book *Kanaries houden als*

Border Fancy canaries at eight weeks of age.

liefhebberij. He writes, "The village (of St. Andreasberg) has some 3800 inhabitants with 800 families, of which 600 are occupied with canary breeding. The women, in particular, take care of the birds. The manufacture of song cages, transport cages, "song cabinets," and other necessary equipment for canary breeding is an important industry. In 1881 St. Andreasberg bred no less than 24,000 Harz canary cocks, which were exported all over the world for high prices, because the quality of these birds was world famous."

For some time now, tourism has ousted the canary industry from its first place as top source of income for the Harz region. In 1885, however, a decline in the industry was already becoming noticeable because of the increasing frequency of infertility and weakness causing the chicks to die while still in the nest. Finally, the quality of their song also declined. Skillful breeders who had not followed a regimented and continuous pattern of inbreeding received high prices for their birds—about 75-100 DM, which represented a considerable amount at that time. The other breeders, however, ran into problems, with exports to England, the United States, and Russia declining sharply. They were able to avoid competition by resorting to the old trick of selling only males, with the tragic consequence of countless hens suffering a violent death. This was actually a matter of honor among the inhabitants of the mountain villages, as it was a way of keeping the breeding of their birds confined to their village. During World War I many inhabitants of St. Andreasberg traveled to the Dutch border, where they swapped their cocks and hens for groceries, particularly coffee! The heyday of St. Andreasberg and the entire Harz is over, but the name "Harz canary" will long remind fanciers of the geographical origin of many great achievements in canary breeding.

Belgian canary breeders have also built an excellent reputation for their world-famous waterslagers, later adding various posture canaries to these achievements as well. The Dutch, too, have not been idle and have enjoyed fame for their color and posture canaries, alongside the Harz canaries and the Waterslagers, as evidenced by the thousands of canaries that are sent all over the world annually. The high quality reputation of the Belgian and Dutch canary exhibitions is not exaggerated, either. Quite often it is these two countries that claim the highest honors and first prizes in international competitions. When Mendel's Law became common knowledge this breeding was perfected. (Mendel was an Augustine priest who lived from 1822 to 1884). In this connection I would like to mention the names of P.J. Helder and C.L.W. Noorduyn. Mr.

Border Fancy hen. The good roundness of the breast in this specimen facilitates the breeding and hatching potential of the bird.

Helder, in particular, has become well known as a breeder of the agate canary. Excellent books have appeared by not only M. Weijling, but also by A. Bartels, who wrote a small work, *Kanaries,* which is still reprinted from time to time. Mr. Weijling's work has been improved and continued by H.J. Veerkamp, who has done much to help every serious-minded aspiring canary breeder with books such as *Handleiding voor de kleurkanariekweker* and *Kanaries kweken kunt u ook.* Many exhibition/competition judges enjoy an international reputation and are often invited to various parts of the world. It is up to each of us to help maintain the level of excellence achieved by our predecessors. I hope then, that this book may stimulate your enthusiasm and help you continue on your chosen path.

Border Fancy canary. Borders exist in all of the standard canary colors; in all cases the color must be of consistent quality and sheen.

An elaborate antique cage, not considered particularly good housing by today's standards.

2: Housing Canaries in Cages and Aviaries

The various canary races have been domesticated so long that they are not very particular about their housing. Of course, this does not mean to imply that we should be satisfied with any little cage or make-shift confinement. Our thoughts should be directed to taking care of these birds, which are so totally dependent upon us, in the best and most responsible way. Only with good and responsible care will our birds be able to enlarge their families with any success. Here again, this does not imply that canaries will only reproduce in large aviaries, because, as we will see later, it is quite likely that most young come from canaries housed in breeding cages. In all the years that I have been involved with cage birds, I have seen quite a variety of strange looking cages, and the funny thing is that even in some of these rather "unavicultural" confinements some of the most beautiful chicks were hatched. Naturally, we should not immediately conclude that the type of housing has no effect on the chances and results of reproduction. On the contrary, if we wish to breed our birds in a responsible manner, then giving them good housing is a first requirement.

What about, then, the very common "canary-in-a-cage?" When we take a look in a pet store, we will be offered a large variety of cage models which are generally built with the inhabitants in mind. Of course, there are some models which we would be well advised not to buy, such as the rather popular "tower" upright cage (probably only

Breeding aviary built in the comfortable setting of a fancier's garden.

suitable for a couple of small tropical birds or a pair of loving budgerigars). In general, the fancy cages with vertical bars are very well suited for canaries. Cages with horizontal bars are only suited for our hook-beaked friends, the parrots and parrakeets. I personally prefer to give each bird as much freedom of movement as possible, but of course that does not mean that we should arbitrarily turn down every cage model. Obviously we cannot be too sure of breeding successes, but the fancier who keeps one canary in a cage is not interested in this anyway; his main concern is to have a good singing canary, and he does not worry himself over procreation opportunities. He very likely does not participate in singing competitions or shows. He really just wants a bird to help create a cozy atmosphere in his home and serve as a topic of conversation! Naturally, I do not want to forget this type of fancier, and I wish to make him

An attic birdroom for Border Fancies.

Commercial canary cage.

aware of the steps he can take in order to keep his canary in good health and assure himself a great deal of enjoyment for many years to come.

CAGES

I am purposely leaving out a complete description of the many models of cages available on the market, since these change (many even improve) from year to year anyway. It has been a long time, fortunately, since a canary fancier placed his canary in a dark little cage barely big enough to allow the bird to turn around! The cages currently available are beautiful, roomy, often finished in chrome or brass and have colorful bottoms made of plastic, plexiglass, etc., thereby avoiding rust, which is a terrific hiding place for bacteria, and preventing spillage of seeds onto the floor. Since the bottom is generally easily separated from the rest of the cage by undoing a few little clamps or by sliding it out, there is no need to catch the bird in order to clean its cage. Cage and bird can be placed on a newspaper while we clean the bottom in a matter of a couple of minutes. Because of the various doors with which a cage is usually equipped, we have easy access to the perches, which should be taken out and sanded clean from time to time. Often the water, seed, and bath containers are affixed to the outside of the cage so that these, too, can be readily cleaned or refilled with a minimum of disturbance to our birds. The glass will need to be cleaned regularly. There are lovely standards available, but I strongly advise against buying one because most cages hung from one will start to swing with the least amount of movement; birds are not particularly fond of having their home turned into an amusement park ride. The cages should not be placed at a low level; a good rule of thumb is that a bird should be able to look down on us, in a matter of speaking!

Very fashionable at the moment are "French" cages, usually antiqued white with a pointy roof, curlicues, and what have you. It is rather difficult to see the bird, but if

Showcage demanded by the International Border Breeder's Association.

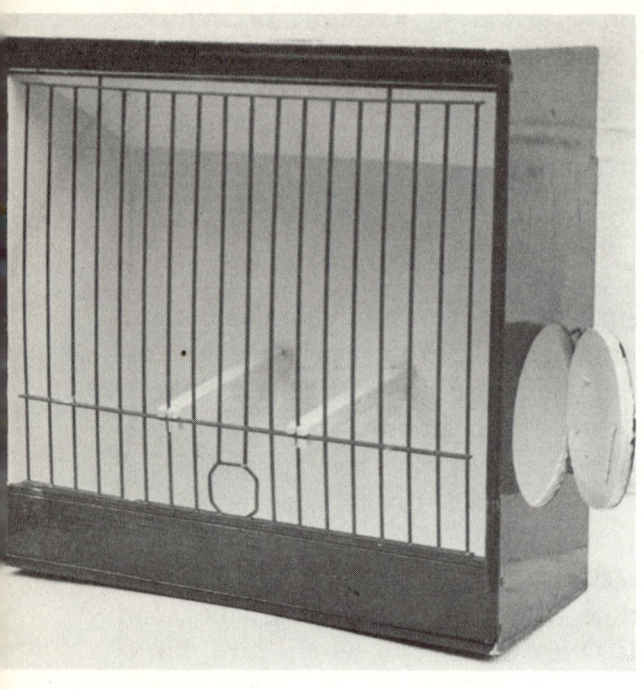

Norwich showcage.

the cage is roomy, there can be no objection to it. Taste is not something that can be disputed anyway. As far as the size of the cage is concerned, let me point out that the posture canaries require more room and therefore need a larger cage than the color and song canaries. Perches should be made of good hardwood (oak, beech) and should not be too thin; a diameter of ½-2 cm is suitable, allowing the bird to encircle his foot around it comfortably. Perches that are too thin promote a too rapid growth of the nails which can cause the bird a great deal of discomfort, and frequent nail-clipping would become necessary. This rapid nail growth can be curbed if the perches are not too smooth and are flattened a little along the top. Using rough sand paper on them once a week will get rid of the smoothness. The best locations for the perches are in front of the seed and water containers. One or two should be toward the top of the cage, being sure, of course, that the bird's head will not touch the top itself. It is very important to provide the birds with a high perch because canaries, like other birds for that matter, prefer to go to roost (sleep) as high up as possible. It is also important not to place too many perches in the cage, because we want to leave enough room for flight and mobility. Obviously perches should not be immediately above another one, since the droppings of the bird on the top perch could soil the bird underneath, providing there is more than one bird in the cage. In any event, it is not a good practice to allow the lower perch to become soiled. It is a good idea, though, to vary somewhat the thickness of the perches, since this variety will provide a certain amount of relaxation to the muscles of the feet and legs.

Commercial canary cage. Keep perches clean and roughened to easily allow the birds a solid grip.

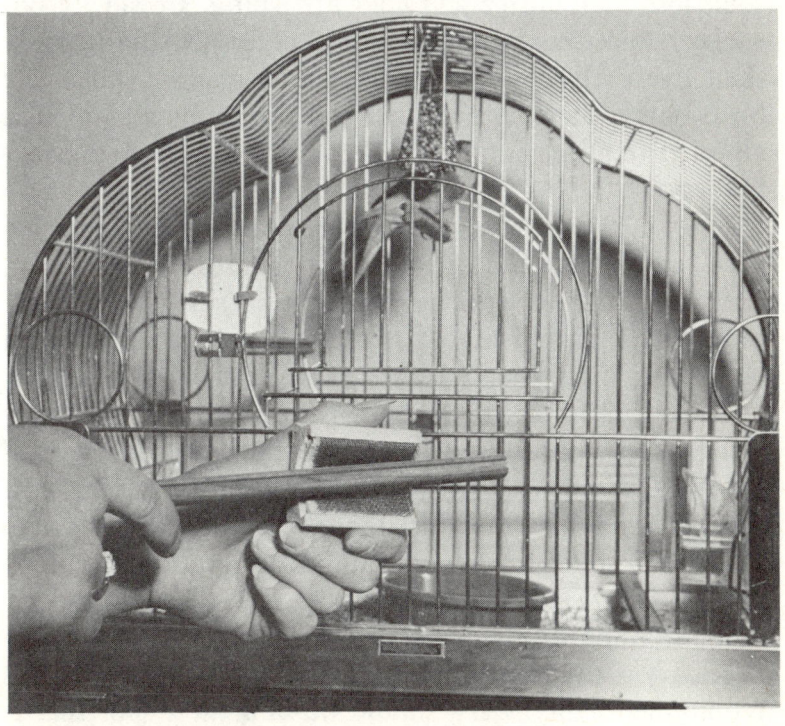

THE LOCATION

Cages (with, for example, a good canary singer, a pair of budgerigars, or tropical birds such as zebra finches and gray singing finches) and aviaries (with perhaps a group of birds) both need light and sun. Rooms and gardens at the north side are totally unsuitable, as well as those little places where we think we can "make a little room" for a small cage. Again, I must stress that light and sun are two essential factors for all birds. If we were able to replace these requirements with fluorescent lighting and sun lamps, our birds would still suffer consequences sooner or later. I do not mean to imply that the birds would not be able to stay alive for a few years; certainly they could, but that is hardly the point. Keeping birds also means, in my opinion at least, keeping their beauty at its peak. The feathers of birds which do not enjoy the benefit of the sun soon lose their luster and color; the birds are slowly but surely reduced to pitiful little heaps of feathers pining away their lives. All too often I have seen expensive and lovely birds housed in such a manner and slowly dying, although all other requirements were taken care of in the best possible way.

It is exactly the same with house plants: no matter how excellent our care and knowledge of plants, if we deny them light, and for many species also the sun, they will lose their beauty and diminish to a stringy bunch of stalks soon doomed to disappear into the garbage can.

One requirement, then, is that the front of the cage or aviary faces south if at all possible. (I am speaking here of the so-called box cage, in which only the front has bars). If this is not feasible, then face the front of the cage or aviary as close to south as possible and rather in a southeasterly than a southwestern direction. It is a good idea to have part of the front of the aviary made of glass, and this is certainly necessary if the front does not face south. Apart from this requirement, the aviary should be built in a spot that is

Border Fancy showcage.

Norwich and Gloster Fancy showcage.

Breeding cages with dividing slides in position.

both pretty and in full view, preferably with some flowers and bushes around it to serve as a lovely frame and background.

This same requirement of facing south, as already stated, applies also to the location of the cage, and here again southeast is preferable to southwest if south is not possible. Indoor aviaries should also face south as much as possible. The whole idea is to allow our birds to enjoy the sunshine for a few hours every day. The suitable locations indoors are also excellent places for indoor plants. With a little artistic insight we can arrange the birds and plants in such a way that the whole will look lovely and natural. Nothing is as disturbing as a bird cage that looks obviously out of place.

THE BOX CAGE

A bird feels most comfortable in a cage that affords him a certain amount of privacy . . . therefore, a cage which is mostly closed. The box cage, which only has bars in the front, with the rest being closed, is many birds' favorite type of cage. It stands to reason that such a cage needs to be placed in a light location. Of course, we do not mean a location that receives the full impact of the sun, because our box cage would soon be transformed into a hot-box! These box cages are ideally suited for breeding because they offer so much privacy to the breeding birds. Later we will discuss the breeding cage, which is a variation of the box cage. Many people place these cages in entrance halls and corridors; there is nothing wrong with this, providing the cage is not subjected to drafts, because birds placed in drafty areas can catch cold, become seriously ill, and ultimately die, even when their feeding and other requirements are completely and properly met. Box cages can also serve as housing during the winter months; they are quite suitable for tropical birds as well.

SAND ON THE CAGE BOTTOM

As mentioned earlier, every well-constructed cage has a sand tray on the bottom that can be slid out for cleaning. Many of the cages sold in pet stores, those made primarily of wire bars, have a bottom part that readily comes apart. It is preferable to first cover the slide-out bottom with a piece of strong paper (such as construction paper or supermarket bags) cut to size. On top of this place the sand, which should be either "shell sand" or grit, both available in various brands at the pet store. A layer of two to three centimeters is sufficient. The sand should be replaced once a week, as should the paper. In order to avoid or at least minimize the kicking of sand out of the cage, it is advisable to affix a 10 cm. high piece of plastic or glass around the bottom of the cage. Many of the decorative cages are made

Paint around the crevices of all breeding equipment with mite killer.

with this convenience already added, but often the tower-type cage is not (this is the one that was more or less condemned previously!). With a cage of this variety, without the glass or plastic "mess preventer," something will have to be improvised.

COVERING THE CAGE

Many bird fanciers have the opinion that a cage should be covered with some kind of cloth during the evening hours and at night. Not every canary is thrilled with this, however. I believe that the best method is to cover just one side, or a part of the top, so that no direct light is shining on the bird. He now has the option to decide for himself whether he wishes to sit in the light or not!

CAUTION IS THE WATCHWORD

When we allow our canaries to fly freely in one of the rooms in our house for a few hours, we must be very sure that all windows and doors are closed and that the windows are covered with drapes. Closed drapes can prevent serious accidents, as otherwise birds cannot see the glass in windows and will crash against it; this could be fatal. Electrical appliances, including an electric range and especially a fan, should not be operating while your bird is in flight. A fan represents a particularly lethal source of danger for a bird that is flying around freely.

Indoor plants and cut flowers can cause a few problems too, since they also present a potential danger to our birds. Cacti can cause some nasty wounds, so it is advisable to either remove the plants from the room or cover them with plastic.

Should the claws of our birds grow faster than is desirable, we can hang a few ceramic perches. These will cause a rapid wearing down of the claws. They are available in every good pet store.

Little mirrors and other toys are fine for budgerigars but should never be placed in a cage housing canaries. As we saw, our cages should be placed in a light spot that is free from drafts. Do not place cages on window sills or high up on a cabinet too close to the ceiling. If we keep several cocks in cages in the same room, then the cages should be placed so that the cocks cannot see each other . . . this for the purpose of keeping their songs up to par. The singing abilities of cocks which can see each other will sharply decline over a short amount of time. Keeping hens which can be seen by

Choosing a show team from quality birds carefully trained for showing.

the cocks but not joined by them is also inadvisable. A cage with one or more canaries should not be placed too close to a TV set, since this is bad for the health of our little feathered friends. Although it is impossible for us to detect the rapid change of dot patterns on a color TV screen, a bird does see this. It is a rather simple deduction to conclude that this is very harmful for their eyes. The farther away from the TV the cage is placed, the less the damage inflicted. Studies on this subject have shown that it is worthwhile to cover the cage when the TV is on if the distance between cage and TV is less than five meters.

Sand on the cage bottom should be either "shell sand" or grit, both available in pet stores.

KEEPING THE CAGE CLEAN

It speaks for itself that the cage must be kept spotlessly clean. This applies to not only the cage, but also to the perches, water and seed feeders, bath, and any holders for cuttlebone and greens. It is best to make a routine habit of this cleaning business; for example, once a week on Saturday afternoon. Once a month everything should be thoroughly disinfected. For this chore we would normally need to remove the birds from the cage. Having an extra little cage on hand can prove to be convenient, if not absolutely necessary. The cage should be cleaned using warm water and later rinsed with cold water, so that disease-carrying bacteria are not given a chance to intrude. The same procedure applies to the various pieces of equipment that belong in the cage. Glass or other types of feeders which are cracked or have pieces broken off should be replaced because cracks are ideal locations for bacteria to gather and sooner or later launch their attack!

BATHS

Wild canaries like to roll around in moist grass. In the early morning when the grass is still covered with dew, this little scene can present the bird enthusiast with a very pleasant sight. In captivity, when we are dealing with domesticated birds, such a sight is very rare. Still, all types of canaries enjoy a water bath. Miniature plastic and metal "bath-houses" are available in pet stores and can be hung over the door opening of the cage. It is very likely that there will be very few days that your canary does not make grateful use of the bath.

When the birds go to a show, they will need to be given a bath a week or so beforehand. Before taking your bird out of his cage, fill two shallow bowls with warm water (about 25°C), dissolving a little mild soap in one of them. A good brand of dishwashing detergent will suffice. Now hold the bird in your hand so that the thumb and forefinger can sup-

A full range of necessary and inexpensive supplies are available at pet shops.

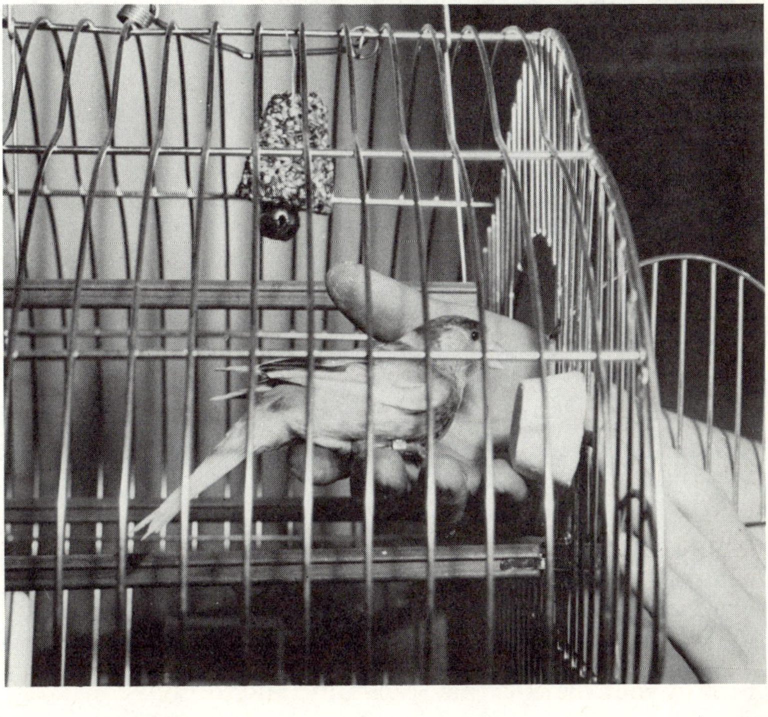

53

A day or two after pairing, the nest pan complete with its lining should be hung onto the small hook at the back of the cage. The exact placing is of relatively little importance, but the most widely accepted position is perhaps midway between the two perches and with the rim at about 1½ to 2 inches above their level. The felt lining is often secured to the pan by means of paste or similar adhesive, but this makes it rather messy to remove at a later date when preparing the nest pan for another lining. A better method is to sew it firmly into position with a strong thread, using the ventilation holes at the sides and bottom of the pan for the purpose.

port his little head and keep it in the right direction. Carefully lower the bird into the soapy water, but be sure that the head is kept dry to ensure that no soap gets into the eyes, nose, or beak. After you have dunked him in this fashion, a few times, wet an old soft-haired shaving brush (or something similar, as shaving brushes are hard to find) in the soapy water and brush the plumage in the direction of the tail. Be sure not to forget the area around the vent.

You can clean the neck and head with a soft sponge. Once again, take care not to get any soap in the eyes, nose, and beak. In order to do a good job in cleaning the wing feathers, you should spread them on the edge of the bowl; the shaving brush will do the rest. You can clean the tail in the same manner, but you will have to be careful in performing all these little operations to avoid accidentally pulling out a feather, which would be rather unfortunate, particularly with show canaries. The clean water is, of course, for rinsing the bird; here again we dunk him a few times and then brush his plumage back into shape with the brush, which you have first thoroughly rinsed in clean water. You can imagine that all this handling has put his feathers a little out of kilter!

We end the operation by drying our bird, which is best accomplished by using a thick towel that has been heated just a little (perhaps in the drier or by hanging it over a radiator for a few minutes). When this task has also been completed, we place our bird in a clean, not too large cage (without sand) in an adequately heated room (never outside in the sun!). Here he should stay until the next day to ensure that he will not catch cold. The room should not, however, be *too* warm, because that will cause his feathers to curl, which, of course, is not the idea. A hair drier can be of service here, but the setting will have to be on low and it should be used with care.

FANCY CLOTHESPINS

The fancy clothespins about 15 cm long made of colorful plastic and used for holding memos and letters can perform many services for us. They can keep a cage door open and serve as a clamp for holding greens, seeding weed stalks, or strips of carrot, to name a couple of uses. They can even serve as perches, with the added advantage that these little resting places can be added or moved practically everywhere in the cage. In the aviary, too, they have their uses, such as clamping greens and seed stalks to the wire or between the nesting boxes. No doubt there are many more possibilities which you will enjoy discovering for yourself.

CARE DURING THE SUMMER MONTHS

Whenever we keep birds, no matter which species, the most important thing to remember is to keep everything as clean as possible. When temperatures are high, it is altogether possible that some of the soft foods (universal food, rearing food, bread that has been soaked in milk or water and greens) may spoil even faster than we would deem possible. High temperatures allow many damaging insects to breed even more rapidly than usual, while the rapid growth of bacteria is also favorably influenced ... favorable for the bacteria, that is! And no matter how strange it may sound, we should not forget the possibility of our birds being subject to sunstroke! That is why inspection, preferably on a daily basis, and absolute cleanliness are so essential.

It is also important that birds that spend the better part of the year indoors be taken outside once in a while, cage and all, during the spring and summer. Do not place the cage in the direct rays of the sun, however, but more or less in the shade, in an area safe from cats, dogs, and other bird enemies. If you keep cats, a constant alertness will very likely be necessary. Many a bird has fallen victim to someone's sweet little pussycat; your birds may well be next! If you are intending to spend some time outside with your birds, they will very much enjoy romping on the grass if you place their cage, minus bottom, on the lawn.

WHAT DO OUR CANARIES REQUIRE FROM US?

From the preceding you will have concluded that canaries that are kept in a cage require very little in the way of care or feeding. These good and often colorful singers certainly do not make many demands upon us! If we provide

Canaries have universal appeal. An enthusiastic interest in canaries is apparent at the active bird market in Moscow.

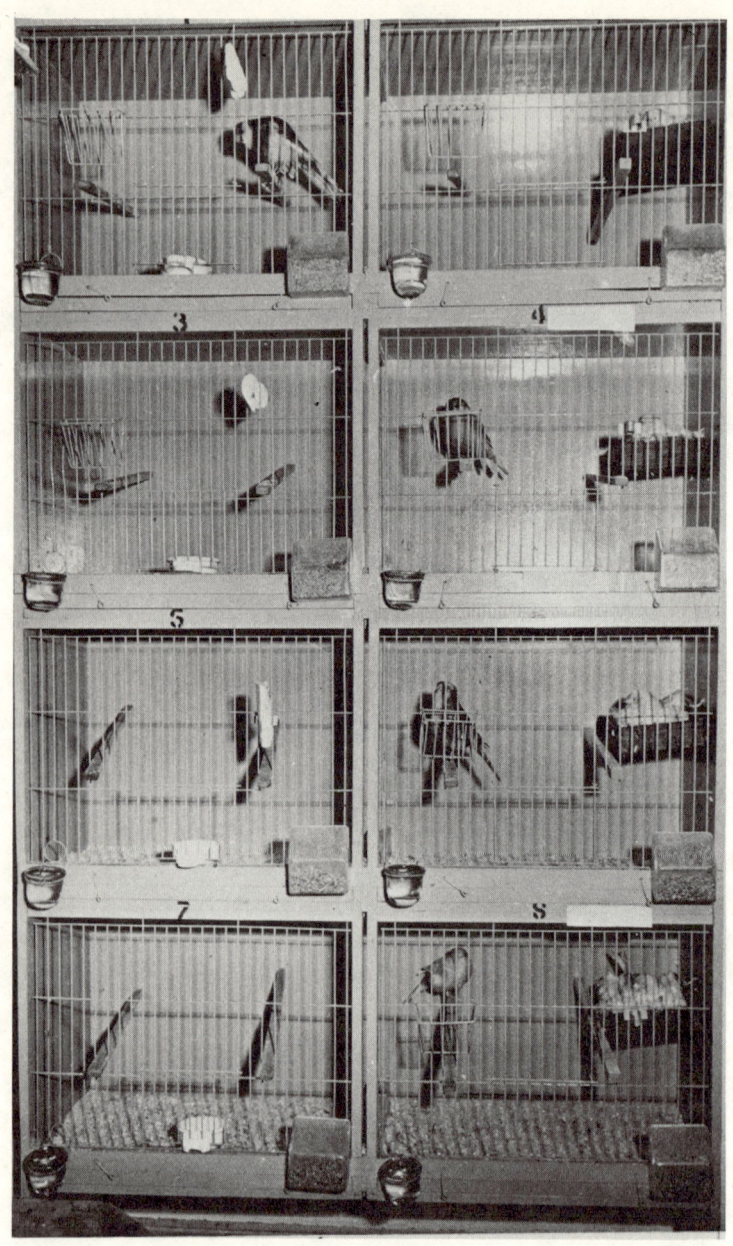
Norwich canaries in breeding cages.

them daily with a feeder of fresh, quality seed, clean drinking and bathing water, weekly treats of spinach, lettuce, or chickweed, and a little calcium (we can hang cuttlebone in the cage as a permanent fixture to take care of that requirement), we might assume that our little canary will be content. Still, I would like to interject a warning here. Although the care and feeding schedule described above is not exactly A-1, I would by far prefer it to the so-called "care" many people give their pet canaries: when supper is served, the canary is given all kinds of goodies such as pieces of vegetables, fruit, meat, cookies, potatoes, bread, sugar, etc. The "funny" thing is that the canary willingly accepts all these treats. But is it good for him? No, of course not. He becomes overweight and lethargic, especially if he is never given the opportunity of flying around the room to exercise a little. But since these "opinions" are quite stuck in the minds of a lot of canary enthusiasts, I will be the last one to say that these practices should be immediately stopped. However, speaking as an ornithologist and aviculturist, I would advise that these 'treats' be gradually eliminated for the sake of your canary's health.

CANARIES IN A COMMUNITY AVIARY

Before I go on to discuss aviaries and their construction, I would like to point out that canaries are certainly not out of place in a community aviary. Since they are not inclined to be aggressive toward fellow species or small exotic birds, housing them in a roomy aviary with other birds is an excellent choice. This does not mean that they never fight a round or two. Those who have kept canaries for some time know that two males in one cage can lead to occasional aggressive acts. On the other hand, if we have three males together there will be no disagreements at all and they will share their lives together in peace and harmony since their basically innocent pursuits and threatening gestures do not mean anything.

American birdcage made in the style of the Regency idea of Chinese bird cages. (Cooper Union Museum.)

On the other side of the coin, we should make sure that the other birds in the aviary do not terrorize the canaries. As a general rule, we should only place in the aviary with our canaries birds which are smaller or of the same size; this implies that they can be housed together with some of the smaller wild song birds. (Caution: permits are required for keeping wild birds!) I personally once kept a bramling in an aviary with canaries, and it turned out to be a proper little terrorist toward certain male canaries and literally mopped the floor with them! All this terrorizing took place on the second day that he was in the aviary. We therefore need to keep an alert eye on our birds so that any hostile attitudes can be detected before it is too late. It speaks for itself that we should be particularly watchful when placing new birds into the aviary. We will later discuss in detail the interesting hybrids that we can produce with wild song birds and canaries.

Most aviculturists are totally against placing canaries together with budgerigars or any other hook-beaked birds. It is not unusual for parrakeets to aim for each other's toes in their acts of aggression, and they will do the same with canaries. Although our hook-beaked friends will adequately defend themselves from each other, canaries are quite timid in this respect, and wounded feet and toes are sure to be the repeated result of this combination of community living. It is not wise to place too many other birds with canaries we are seriously considering breeding, because canaries, like most birds, like peace and quiet during the breeding season.

In one area—perches—canaries are fussy. In the preceding pages I have already said quite a lot about perches. Canaries, like other birds, prefer to sit as high up as possible, so it is important to place a more than sufficient number of perches in high locations to avoid evening quarrels among canaries choosing their spot for the night. These perches should be located close to the wall, and they should all be placed at the same height. It is unlikely that the settling

Roller canaries in their cages. These birds occupy an optimum location in the room to receive proper ventilation and light.

down proceedings will ever be completely peaceful, but this should eliminate most of the problems! I would point out once again that elsewhere in the aviary the perches are placed in such a manner that a bird sitting on one will not soil a bird sitting below. Allow for a variety in the thickness of the perches, ranging from ½ to 2 cm. in diameter.

It is desirable to place several water and seed feeders in the aviary to avoid quarrels. Nothing is as important in a

Birdroom and aviary, known as "the shelter and flight."

community aviary as peace and tolerance. If these elements are not present in the aviary, there is little or no chance of achieving good breeding results, and I assume that this is the goal of most bird fanciers.

A community aviary should be equipped with several choices in **nesting boxes** or nesting pans, preferably twice as many nesting facilities as there are pairs of birds. Do not hang the nesting boxes and pans too close together though, again to avoid arguments.

AVIARIES

There are various ways of keeping canaries. If we are not particular about the color factor in breeding . . . in other words, we do not want to breed first-class offspring to take part in exhibitions . . . we can build an aviary and house in it several canaries along with various other birds. Of course we can also choose to keep in an aviary these color canaries that are our particular favorites. This means, however, that we should keep only with homozygous or pure-breeding

Garden aviary illustrating how part of the front may be constructed of glass for natural lighting.

birds if we want to know exactly which colors each bird will pass on to the next generation. If we place a random collection of birds together, we will obviously get a potpourri of colors and combinations of colors which will be useless to us and will not allow us to determine the colors of their offspring.

The aviary is an ideal housing facility providing we use it in a wise manner. If we are really first-class color canary breeders and therefore not satisfied with just one color, we are left with only one possibility: we will need to build more aviaries. Each aviary, then, will produce just one particular color. These aviaries need not be all that large, but it would follow that it is both important and understandable that there should be sufficient room to allow freedom of movement for the inhabitants. The following notes should help give the do-it-yourselfer an ideal aviary, which you no doubt will adapt to your own specifications. In the first place, a good aviary consists of inside and outside areas known as the shelter and flight. First let's talk about the building and equipping of the flight.

Border Fancy Clear Yellow. Fine outline; the character of the head, neck and body are emphasized for the breed. Well elevated legs show the 60-degree posture. Very beautiful in all respects (except the tail end).

This Birdroom interior has a neat and uniform arrangement of the cages, most of which are the 'treble-breeder' type having a smaller center compartment which is useful when pairing one cock bird to two hens. This photograph was taken out of the breeding season when the cages were being used for general stock accommodation.

LOCATION

As far as the location is concerned, pick a spot that allows the front of the aviary to face a southerly direction as much as possible. If this is not possible, then direct the front to face as close to south as possible, preferably southeast rather than southwest. Even if the aviary front faces south, it is still advisable to construct part of the front from glass. Choose a spot in the garden which will allow us to enjoy our aviary as much as possible, preferably one surrounded by flowers, bushes, and shrubs. Nothing is as ugly as an aviary standing by itself without a natural background into which to blend.

MATERIAL

It is not a good idea to use only wood in the construction of an aviary meant for canaries. Sooner or later we are likely to be visited by mice, rats, weasels, or our neighbor's pussy-cat. I won't go into the damage that these animals can do, but it will suffice to say that it is obviously important that our aviary is built so that these injurious animals cannot intrude. It is best to build the foundation of concrete; the sides can be erected using wooden 2x4's, which can be strengthened with metal stripping, though this is not absolutely necessary for the aviary housing canaries. On top of the foundation we should next build a little wall about 30-40 cm. high. At that same height we build the floor, again preferably from concrete (particularly in the night shelter) though kiln-dried or creosote-treated posts and planks can also be used; tiles, too, can be useful here. For the closed walls and inner dividing panels, our best choice is asbestos sheets. The roof can also be constructed of asbestos. Although a further covering is not necessary, it looks very attractive to finish the roof with roofing tiles or slate. The roof should be built at a shallow angle. If the aviary is built against an existing fence (if this is permissible in your area), then the roof should extend just a

Garden aviary with birdroom in a "naturally" landscaped surrounding where shade and sunlight are available.

Crested canary. Heavily feathered and large-crested, this clear-bodied grizzled crest shows the important features of the breed.

Opposite:
Scotch Fancy canary.

little to avoid water from collecting where it is joined to the fence; a strip of asphalt or tar paper can do a lot to eliminate this problem as well. Apart from the materials mentioned above, we will need sturdy wire mesh (approx. 1.5 cm. diameter openings), wire strands, nails, and glass. For the half-covered area of the outer aviary (flight) it is best to use either wired glass or safety glass. Generally a plastic or aluminum gutter is also necessary or at least very useful.

SHAPE AND SIZE

The size of a chicken or duck coop is determined by the number of inhabitants one plans to keep, but with an aviary it is the other way around: first we determine by the space and location available what size our aviary can be, and from that the number of birds. If we have ample space, we can try to keep and breed birds on a community basis (several males and several females), but with all birds of the same color in order to maintain pure (homozygous) birds; I am not directly in favor of this, however. As far as the shape of the aviary is concerned, I would advise the following: stick to conventional straight lines, at least to the extent that our aviary will fit into its surroundings. The contents of the aviary should remain the focal point, so various means of embellishing the aviary, such as little towers and domes, are generally not a good idea. An aviary that blends in with nature by adding all kinds of flowers and shrubs is generally a bigger success. Never make the aviary too low: the height of the front should be 2-2½ meters (approx. 8 ft.) as a minimum.

LAYOUT

If we divide the aviary into three parts, we will be able to make an entirely open area, a covered area, and a completely closed-in area . . . the night shelter. The night shelter could possibly be eliminated if the covered area is only open at the sides, against which the nesting boxes can be

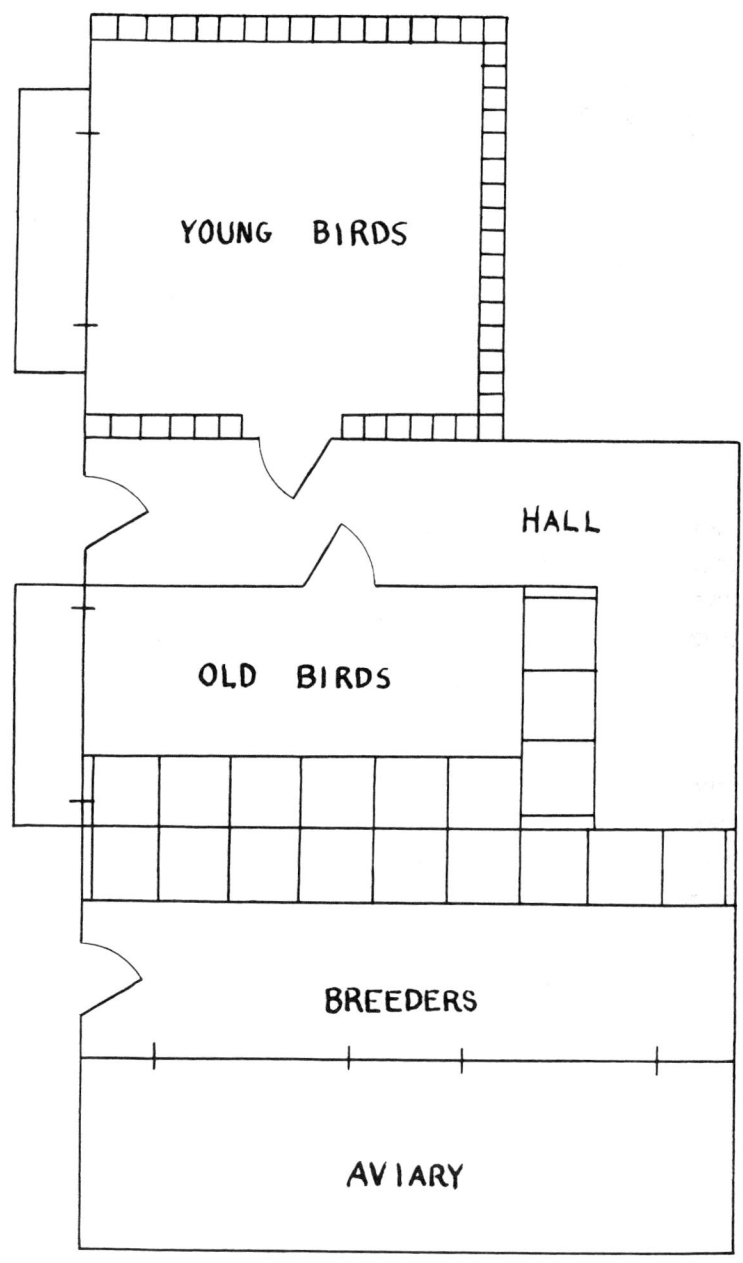

Floor plan of an indoor aviary.

A typical canary's nest built in a 'nest pan'. The usual clutch is four (as shown here) or five eggs.

Newly independent, these two young green canaries have just been weaned. It is still rather difficult to ascertain the sex of young canaries. As a general rule young cocks are more bold in appearance and livelier in action than the young hens.

hung up. Personally, I have found that most canaries like to breed in the night shelter, providing this is well lighted. This can be readily achieved by a window in one of the sides that could possibly even be opened during the summer. There is nothing wrong with this, providing there is a plentiful supply of fresh air (not a draft!) coming into the shelter. A completely free-standing aviary (not one that is built against an existing fence or garage) can be built with the nesting boxes affixed against the back wall on specially installed wooden slats or furring strips. Many fanciers prefer completely open aviaries, and these certainly seem to promote the desire to breed.

This particular aviary, then, consists only of two compartments, an open part and a covered part, with a few large half-open breeding boxes or specially made night shelter boxes substituting for the night shelter. When we install a few perches inside such a night shelter box (which consists of two side walls, a back wall, and a roof and measures about 60-80 cm. long with a height of 30 cm), these should not, of course, be directly over one another, since the birds on the top perch could then easily soil the birds below with their droppings.

THE OPEN AREA

Our canaries should not be outside during the winter, so it is essential that our aviary has a closed night shelter which we can supply with heat or a night shelter box as described in the previous paragraph. However, the temperature in the night shelter proper must not fall below the freezing point; if it does we will need to move our birds indoors or perhaps into an attic room. The completely open part of the aviary serves to toughen our birds and keep them "in color"; furthermore, it gives them a feeling of freedom which will only enhance their desire to breed. The entire part is built with iron poles or treated 2x4's and wire . . . in other words, the walls and roof are all made of

Garden shed converted to accommodate breeding canaries.

Garden shed converted to birdroom, a measure "handy" fanciers may wish to undertake to provide optimum space at minimal expense.

Border Fancy canary. This self-blue, mated to a self-green, would produce greens and blues in equal proportions among their progeny.

Lizard canary. The oldest of all canary breeds. This clear-capped gold shows the breast markings well, but little can be seen of the 'spangling' on the back.

wire. It is preferable to have a dirt floor in this area, allowing plants and bushes to be planted. When, finally, the perches have been installed, our canaries will have plenty of resting and pairing places and can unrestrictedly enjoy the sun and an occasional shower.

THE COVERED AREA

This area has a water-tight roof and perhaps an asbestos back wall separating it from the night shelter, with the rest being constructed from wire. This part could also have a dirt floor, though one of cement blocks covered with a generous layer of sand is also excellent. If we choose a concrete floor, however, the shrubbery will have to consist of small bushes and fresh willow branches placed in tubs and other large planters and will need to be replaced as necessary. Of course, this area will also need to be equipped with perches. These perches, as well as those in the open area, need to be cleaned regularly, though those in the outside aviary will probably be pretty well taken care of by the rain. Perhaps when you water the plants you could hose them off at the same time. In any event, a regular check on the perches will do no harm.

In this area we should use safety glass that can be seen by the birds so they will not fly into it. Plexiglass is also often used.

THE CLOSED AREA

We build a tiny "entrance hall" with double doors in the front of the closed area in an attempt to avoid losing any birds when we go in and out of the aviary. Once in this little hall, we naturally close the outer door before opening the inner one, which brings us to the night shelter. This area is divided in half horizontally. The top half is the actual night shelter. The bottom half is again divided into two, vertically this time; one part is used as a pairing room, quarantine station, confinement area for punishing trouble-

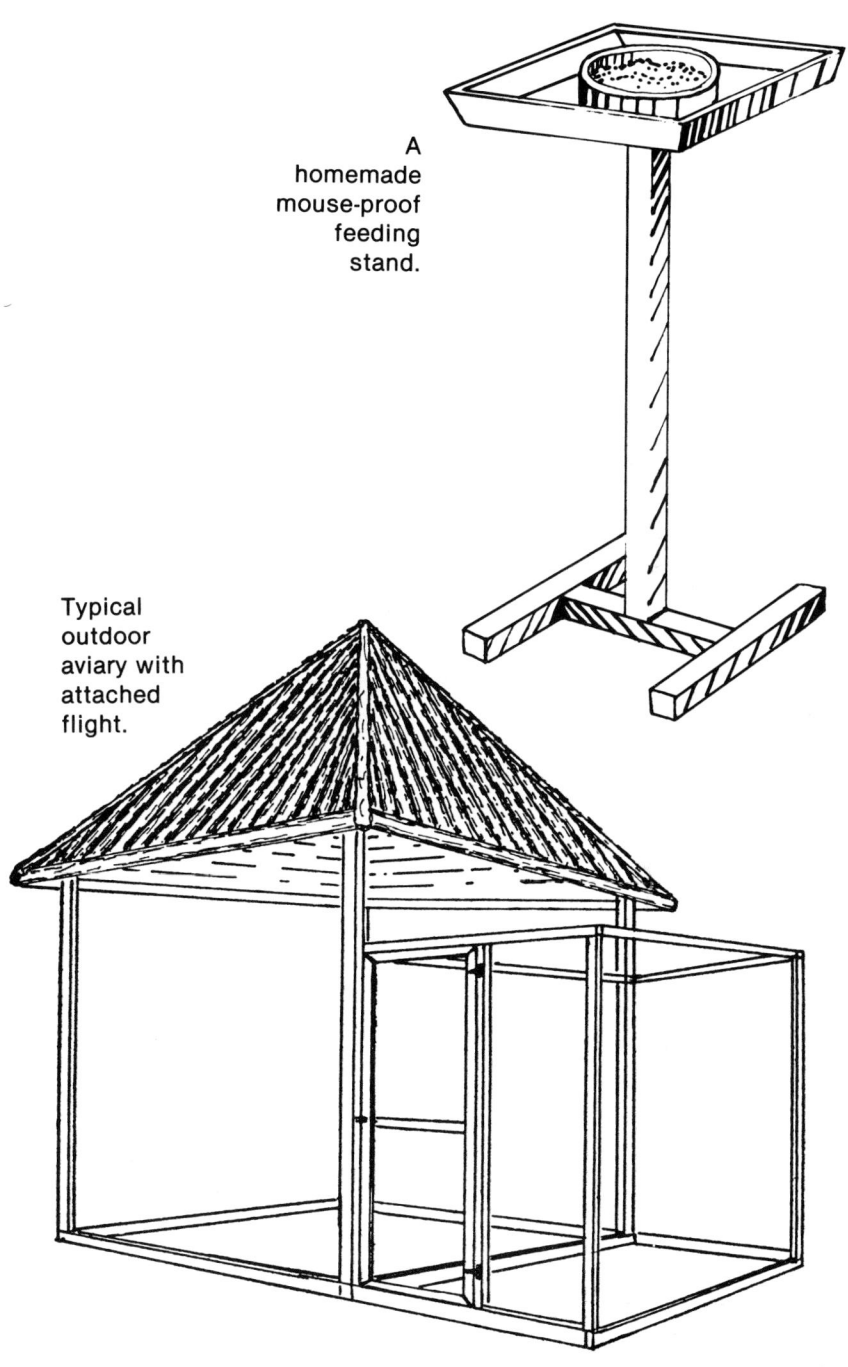

A homemade mouse-proof feeding stand.

Typical outdoor aviary with attached flight.

Young Border Fancy chicks three weeks old and just leaving the nest.

A nest of chicks at about ten days old gaping for food.

makers, observation room, etc., and the other part is used as a storage space for nesting boxes, perches, water and seed hoppers, dishes, etc. The floor of the bottom half should be made of either absestos, concrete or tiles, as should the floor of the night shelter, though this is to be covered with a 6-8 cm.-thick (about 3″) layer of sand and grit. The sides of the night shelter are made of wire.

GENERAL REMARKS

I would like to make a few more remarks regarding the building of the aviary. When making the foundation, be sure to bury the wire in the ground to help keep out mice and rats. Adding wire to the concrete floor during pouring will help prevent cracking. Be sure the entire edge of the roof extends at all points. If you intend to divide your aviary into compartments and keep lovebirds, budgerigars, or other parrots in one of these, be sure to use double wire for the partitions since our hook-beaked friends, which spend a lot of time up against the wire, think nothing of grabbing a canary toe or foot that happens to be sticking through the wire ... with obvious tragic results not needing further explanation. The asbestos you use can be painted if you like, but then be sure to use child-safe paint, since these paints do not contain any harmful ingredients. The wire and any other metal can be painted green if you prefer, but of course everything must be completely dry before any canaries are placed inside the aviary. Whitewashing is not a good idea because most whitewashes contain some harmful elements and sooner or later most will begin to peel. Pieces that are then picked up by the birds can be harmful to their health.

BIRD ROOM

This is really nothing more than an outside aviary erected indoors or on an enclosed porch. The construction is basically the same, using wire for the windows and the little entrance hall.

Including greens in the canaries' diet is very important during breeding season.

Border Fancy canary. A self-blue. As can be seen, the 'blue' is really more of a slate-grey with quite a mixture of brown.

Yorkshire canary. A blue variegated white.

Couple of baby Gloster Fancy canaries.

The bird room is used a great deal by breeders of color and song canaries; it is also excellent for use with tropical and sub-tropical birds. I am thinking here also of the possibility of keeping a few rare birds together with our canaries, providing, of course, they are compatible species. Expensive birds in particular, such as the larger hummingbirds, various Australian grass finches, etc., are really done justice when kept in such a facility.

The belief that the bird room is found only among the more experienced bird fanciers has been disproved in recent years. Quite often a bird room will be found to be even more efficient and appropriate than an outside aviary, especially for those who are able to use one room in their home for just this hobby. It goes without saying that some prior planning will do much to help make our bird room effective and enjoyable. The floor should consist of tiles covered with a layer of sand, which must be replaced regularly. We would also want to enhance our bird room with as much natural shrubbery as possible; miniature trees and bushes can be placed in tubs or large pots. A little insight can help us recreate a lovely piece of nature right inside our home!

INDOOR AVIARY

The indoor aviary has also become quite popular, particularly among fanciers who do not wish to breed only color or posture canaries but just wish to keep and breed some birds on a more casual basis, even though it does lend itself for breeding a specific bird type. The indoor aviary is actually a small aviary that we place in a room in our home. The equipping of it parallels that of the outside aviary. Many people confuse the indoor aviary with the bird room. Unlike the bird room, however, the indoor aviary is simply a small aviary that is placed in a den, for example, while the bird room utilizes an entire room not used for anything else.

Bird fanciers who do not have a garden or a large house often find the indoor aviary to be an ideal solution. I have seen indoor aviaries that were really beautiful and in which, furthermore, birds bred successfully even though children played daily on the floor and at a table less than a meter away from the several nesting boxes. Of course breeding results are generally better if such an aviary is placed in a room where it is more peaceful. One can also arrange several of the extra large breeding cages in a circle so that they all empty into a community flight. In short, there are

A nice brood of young Border Fancies.

Soon to leave the nest, these young Gloster Fancy **canaries are** about eighteen days old.

enough possibilities that I am confident any serious-minded canary fancier who has a little initiative and skill will be able to responsibly house and care for his birds.

SHRUBBERY

Many outside aviaries, as well as other types of housing, are very poor in the area of shrubbery. One seems to assume, quite incorrectly, that our canaries can suffice if we supply them with a number of artificial perches. However, we should keep in mind that our birds like to spend a lot of time outside in the sunshine but not necessarily in the direct rays of the sun. There is no better way to fulfill this desire than by supplying them with ample shrubbery. I feel, therefore, that one requirement of an outside aviary is that there be plenty of greenery, but without hampering the flying space. A natural arrangement of plants and bushes will also quickly stimulate our birds to breed; it gives them a sense of protection and privacy. This is why evergreens are also highly recommended, and they do not need to be all that expensive. We can usually find some bargains, if we feel so inclined, by inquiring about some of the slightly "out of shape" bushes at the nursery. In the covered part of the inner aviary it would be preferable to place a few attractive dead trees in addition to the necessary artificial perches. The following is a brief listing of those trees and bushes that are suitable for planting in the aviary.

Silver fir (*Abies alba,* also *Picea abies*). The needles of the silver fir are a shiny dark green on the top side and there are two bluish white stripes running along the bottom side. The buds are light brown and do not feel sticky since they do not secrete any resin. The needles are 2-3 cm long and are individually attached. This tree is an evergreen that is particularly attractive and decorative while still young and will do well even when planted in poor, sandy soil.

Nordmann fir (*Abies nordmanniana*). This fir has needles that are striking, shiny, 2-3 cm. long and are attached in a

Border Fancy cock.

Yorkshire canary. A clear buff, standing 'at ease'.

Yorkshire canary. A cinnamon variegated buff showing all sorts of faults in this particular photograph.

Border Fancy canary, a buff hen.

brush-like arrangement. The egg-shaped buds also do not secrete resin. This fir is an ideal aviary plant in its young form. It originated in Asia Minor and the Caucasus but is grown everywhere.

Douglas fir (*Pseudotsuga taxifolia* or *P. menziesii*). The needles of this fir tree form two rows and are 18-33 mm. long. They are a lovely light green on top, while the underside is a grey-green. There are irregularly placed little resin knobs on the bark. This fir tree can grow to an enormous size, as high as 90 meters or even more and to 4 meters in diameter. Naturally, only young trees are suitable for the aviary. This tree originated in North America but is grown in various parts of the world.

Spruce fir (*Picea excelsa*). The needles, which are about 2 cm. long, are individually attached to each branch. Dark green in color, the buds have no resin. Branches grow right to the bottom of the straight trunk, particularly in specimens subject to direct light. Also contributing to its popularity is the fact that it is a very hardy evergreen.

European larch (*Larix decidua*). The soft, light green needles (up to 30 mm. long) fall off in the fall and are placed in small groups in cuplike sheaths. This tree will even do well in the poor soil often found inside the aviary.

Scotch pine (*Pinus silvestris*). This tree, which is so common in sandy soil areas and on moors, etc., will understandably also do well inside the aviary, particularly the small specimens under a meter high. It is an evergreen. The firm needles grow in small bunches (two needles), are bluish green in color, and can grow to 8 cm. in length. The bud is reddish brown and seldom secretes resin.

Austrian pine (*Pinus nigra*). This is often used as a decorative tree. The needles can grow as long as 15 cm. and stand in pairs; they are blackish green in color. The bud produces resin. Young specimens in particular are very attractive.

American arborvitae (*Thuja occidentalis*). This tree is par-

Border Fancy canary. A yellow hen.

ticularly suitable for being grown as a hedge in the aviary, especially in a community aviary with tropical birds. The scallop-shaped leaves are placed in a cross design. In earlier days, girls used to place a twig from this tree inside a handkerchief to enjoy the pleasant scent that can be brought out by rubbing it a little. These twigs are dark green on top and light green underneath. The American arborvitae can grow to 15 meters tall. It originated in North America, as indicated by its name, but is grown in various other places in great numbers. Obviously only young specimens are suitable for use in the aviary.

Oriental arborvitae (*Thuja orientalis*). The leaves are arranged in the same symmetry as the American arborvitae. Both sides of the needles are green. This tree originally came from Japan and China but is grown in great quantity elsewhere. It can also be found in the wild in Persia.

English holly (*Ilex aguifolium*). This evergreen shrub can grow to a tree of some 7 meters in height. The leaves, which grow to 7 cm. long and are attached to a short stem, are egg-shaped to oval; leaves have rounded teeth and are green. This plant does well when pruned and can often be seen pruned into various shapes. We generally plant male and female holly shrubs together so that they will produce the red berries much loved by the birds. The flowers are small and attached to short stems. This plant does best when located in a sunny spot where the ground is not too dry.

Common boxwood (*Buxus sempervirens*). This evergreen, which originated from the areas around the Mediterranean, is an excellent choice for the aviary. The little oval leaves grow to about 2 cm. and have a leathery feel; they are dark green on the top and whitish green underneath. A hedge about one meter long will do very nicely in the aviary. Many tropical birds, particularly several weaver varieties, like to build their nests in such a hedge.

Common privet (*Ligustrum vulgare*). This species, which

comes from southern Europe and Asia Minor, generally loses its leaves in winter. The sturdy, lancet-shaped leaves, which grow to about 8 cm. in length, are an excellent food for various parrot varieties, such as the cockatiel. This tree offers ideal nesting places for tropical birds, and our canaries enjoy its protection on especially sunny days. Its wood is hard. In April and May little white flowers bloom in small hanging bunches. The common privet is one of the most popular aviary plants, a fact easily understood when one considers its many favorable characteristics.

False spirea (*Sorbaria sorbifolia*). This shrub comes from Siberia and can reach a height of three meters, so small specimens are ideal for the aviary. The yellowish white flowers are arranged in bunches.

Japanese spirea (*Spirea japonica*). Because of its numerous branches, this spirea also makes an ideal aviary plant. It loses its leaves in the fall. As indicated by the name, it originated in Japan. The oval leaves are wedge-shaped at their base and grow to 10 cm. long and 4 cm. across.

Snowberry (*Symphoricarpos albus*). This North American shrub reaches a height of about two meters and loses its round or oval leaves in the fall. Some tropical birds like to make their nests on the knotty branches. The round white berries remain on the shrub during the winter and are gratefully devoured by blackbirds, pheasants, and quail.

Common juniper (*Juniperus communis*). This evergreen can grow to a height of 10 meters and more. They can take on various attractive shapes and are generally a decorative addition to the landscape, be it woods, moors, or planted forest. It looks very good in the aviary. Its needles are arranged in small wreaths in groups of three. It will even do well in poorer soil.

English ivy (*Hedera helix*). This beautiful and very useful plant often grows up the trunks of oak and beech trees. It is ideal for the aviary and remains green all year round. If the

Gloster Fancy canary, a Corona cock.

aviary has a back wall of stone or concrete, it offers a perfect background on which to leave the ivy. The leaves of young shoots and those that grow along the ground have three to five lobes. At the branches the leaves become oval, diamond-shaped and lancet-shaped. The leaves have a leathery feel and are veined in white. The ivy bears round bluish black berries that are much enjoyed by many birds. Tropical birds

This is a Border belonging to a breeder who prefers the colony system.

will nestle in the ivy, particularly if we place a few nests made of string among the branches.

European elderberry (*Sambucus nigra*) and common elderberry (*Sambucus canadensis*). Both elderberries are hardy shrubs with strongly scented flowers arranged in bunches. The leaves are dark green, and the black berries—which are greatly enjoyed by many different types of birds—are also edible by man. An important thing about the elderberry is that it is often pestered by aphids. The birds will thoroughly check all the branches looking for aphids and little spiders. If we give a couple of aphid-infested branches to our birds once in a while, this will provide them with a few hours of real feasting! These branches are almost essential to our tropical birds during the breeding period.

Oregon holly-grape (*Mahonia aquifolium*). This evergreen shrub from North America is commonly grown. It grows to a height of about one meter, which makes it an ideal size for the aviary. Its bullet-shaped dark blue berries are enjoyed by the birds, which helps make it a good choice. The leaves have rather prickly teeth and are oval. They are a beautiful red in the summer and blackish red in the winter. The Oregon holly-grape will do well in almost any location and any soil.

Rhododendron (*Rhododendron ponticum*). Rhododendrons come in many varieties, all of them beautiful. Because their leaves are quite hard, they are not dangerous for canaries and tropical birds, in contrast to parrakeets, which you probably know cannot keep their little beaks off anything! Studies have shown that practically all rhododendron varieties have poisonous leaves, but they do not present any danger in the aviary housing only canaries and tropical birds. The wild varieties do quite well as undergrowth plants. Rhododendrons require very little in the way of care, although a little humus will do much to promote their growth and flowering.

English hawthorn (*Crataegus monogyna*). This shrub sheds its leaves and has a thick branch network in which many birds like to build their nests. The leaves have three to seven lobes with deep indentations. Birds like the red, bullet-shaped berries. This shrub also demands very little, though a little sun is always welcome.

Climbing rose (*Rosa multiflora*). This climbing rose is very well suited as an aviary plant. The small leaves are oval in shape and clearly indented. The trunk will creep

Norwich canary, variegated.

horizontally or climb vertically as the environment allows. The thorns are saber-shaped and arranged in pairs. This plant is often used as a hedge and would be excellent in a roomy aviary.

European hornbeam (*Carpinus betulus*). This species makes an ideal hedge in which the birds—I am again thinking of small exotic birds—will like to build their nests. The oval leaves are clearly doubly indented and attached to short little stems. The leaves turn a beautiful brownish yellow in the winter. Since they take a long time before they finally fall off, they do lend some protection from the wind and rain. When temperatures drop well below the freezing point, however, the leaves will drop quite quickly.

As a tree, the European hornbeam can grow to a height of 10-14 meters.

Apart from all the above, there are several other choices (actually the choices are endless)—such as: all *Prunus* (cherry) species, the mock orange (*Philadelphus coronarius*), the *Viburnum* species, and sea buckthorn (*Hippophae rhamnoides*). Also good are various *Vaccinium* species, such as the high bush blueberry, whortleberry, or swamp blueberry (*Vaccinium corymbosum*), the cranberry (*Vaccinium macrocarpon*), the low bush blueberry (*Vaccinium pennsylvanicum* or *Vaccinium augustifolium*), and the cowberry or foxberry (*Vaccinium vitis-idaea*). Then there are various *Genistra* species, including African broom (*Genistra monosperma*), creeping broom (*Genistra pilosa*), dwarf broom (*Genistra sagittalis*), and dyer's greenweed (*Genistra tinctoria*). Also, don't forget the *Cotoneaster* species. Grass sods are also good. If we water the grass regularly, we will very likely often see our birds frolicking on it . . . a very pleasant sight indeed! Tropical birds enjoy grass sods, too, and will seek out insects and the like in it. Many birds lie in the grass to sunbathe.

MAINTENANCE

The sand we sprinkle on the aviary floor will need to be replaced regularly, while the soil will need to be dug up on a regular basis, the frequency depending upon the size of the aviary and the number of inhabitants. At least once every spring all perches, sleeping quarters, and any other little hiding places should be cleaned and disinfected. All shrubbery and any other natural perches for canaries must be pruned whenever necessary and any rotting or dying pieces removed from the aviary. All woodwork and metal in the aviary must be hosed off, and any dead plants should be replaced.

If it is at all possible, it would be a good idea to house our birds in flight cages temporarily, allowing us the oppor-

Yorkshire canary.

tunity to really clean both the interior and exterior and repair any leaks, drafty cracks, faults in the wire, locks, etc. . . . in short, bringing everything back into top form. Should you decide to have your birds spend the winter indoors, including winter-hardened birds that could spend the winter outside, this would be the ideal time to check and repair everything at your leisure. If we repeat this procedure each year, it is most unlikely that we will be surprised by a great many problems at any one time. During the winter, when we do not breed our birds anyway, we must be sure to do a thorough cleaning job on the nesting boxes, because these objects in particular are favorite breeding grounds of bacteria, so diseases could easily develop a stronghold here. Besides these nesting boxes, we should also take care of feed hoppers, water dishes and fountains, any birdbaths, etc. The feed and water hoppers should be placed in such a way that the bird fancier has easy access to them without disturbing his birds too much. During the breeding season in particular it is desirable to give our birds as much peace and quiet as possible so they can watch their eggs or young virtually undisturbed.

Keep your aviary as clean as you can . . . both you and your birds will benefit.

Roller youngsters ready for their first "worldly" adventures.

3: CARE AND FEEDING OF THE CANARY

When we keep birds, we should make it a point to see that they are located in a peaceful spot or very little will come of breeding or the rearing of the young. They prefer a restful, quiet environment and very much dislike being startled. When observing experienced bird keepers, we will see that they enter the aviary in a calm, quiet manner, more often than not talking to their birds. The birds become accustomed to their keeper very quickly this way and will not fly around anxiously whenever the keeper is checking the feed and water containers. During the period when there are young birds in the nests, he will be able to inspect the nesting boxes without causing a calamity. In fact, many canaries become so tame that they do not even object to having their keeper stick his hand in the nest to check on the eggs or the chicks . . . the breeding bird will merely jump onto the edge of the nest and calmly observe the actions of the keeper. In order to achieve this degree of tameness, however, the bird keeper will need to follow a routine with which the birds will become familiar and which will have a calming effect upon them. As an example, if we are in the habit of generally wearing a cap of some sort, we should make it a point to always wear it, particularly during the breeding period. If the birds see you entering the aviary without your usual hat, this in itself can cause some unrest among them, because they will have ascertained that something is not quite right. In this connection there is another example I would like to mention: many show judges wear

Canary nestpans and nestbox suitable for Norwich canary.

eyeglasses, so if you breed show birds but don't wear glasses, do buy eyeglass frames without lenses and wear these whenever you are taking care of your birds. This may well help prevent your birds from becoming jumpy at that crucial time . . . during the show!

The above does not intend to imply that breeding cannot take place indoors where it may be a little noisy at times. On the contrary, the canary has been bred by man for hundreds of years and has, as a consequence, become very accustomed to man, although he will always remain sensitive to the out-of-the-ordinary loud noises or to observers with rather wildly flailing arms! Yet even to these things a canary can become accustomed, but in the meantime a few breeding seasons will have come and gone. After that, however, some breeding success can be counted on, even in such a rowdy environment. You understand, of course, that these are less than ideal conditions, and you will very likely have one or more breeding seasons which produce nothing but ill. Personally, I am against allowing a lot of interested parties to observe the breeding birds during that season; it only tends to make the birds restless, whereby they neglect their breeding and rearing duties, with an end result that could cost many young or eggs. It only takes one alarmed bird to instigate a general panic! The results need not be explained to you, I am sure.

In this regard, I would like to say a few words about the catching of the birds. I am sure we are all agreed that catching birds, regardless of the species, is a nerve-wrecking task which must at all times be performed in a controlled manner and with a certain amount of planning. Never lose your patience and never try to catch all of the inhabitants of an aviary in one session. Use a net with medium-sized holes. The opening of the net should have a diameter of about 28 cm. and the net itself should be about 35 cm. deep.

Any good pet store will have this kind of net in stock, but we can also easily make one ourselves from some smooth material, such as an old sheet. The pole should not be too long—about 50 cm. is more than long enough. Before you start catching the birds, you should remove all of the seed and water containers, breeding boxes, etc., so that these will not get in your way. The best and safest way to catch your birds is in flight. They can also be caught when they are hanging against the wire, but be very careful, because if you should happen to accidentally knock a canary with the edge of the net, he may fail to survive it. This is why it is imperative that we cover the opening ridge of the net with cotton or foam rubber. The most important thing to remember is to remain calm and under no circumstances lose your patience. As already stated, it is also important not to catch all our birds at one time. I think it is better to spend two 5-minute sessions at catching them than one 10-minute session. A break of 15 minutes between sessions is a must. Needless to say, this catching business is very scary to your birds; any long sessions will unnecessarily exhaust them. It would not be the first time that a bird keeper found one or more dead canaries (or other birds) on the ground a day after such a catching session, victims of too much tension and total exhaustion.

Canaries that are kept in cages should be caught by hand. Stick your hand in the cage and wait a moment until the birds have quieted down again; then catch them in a fast but controlled action. It is best not to wear a long-sleeved shirt for this operation, as buttons may be caught between the bars.

There are also several comments I would like to make with regard to care.

Since canaries do not provide us with many care problems, even a beginner will find it possible to keep these charming birds and breed them. Those who are satisfied with simply keeping a canary in a fancy cage certainly do not need to be well-informed aviculturists in order to keep their birds in good health. Providing certain requirements are taken care of in a responsible manner, it is unlikely the pet owner will be faced with any unpleasant surprises. First of all, our birds must be suitably housed. Every day, regardless of the type of housing you have provided your birds, their drinking water must be freshened. If we have large aviaries with many inhabitants, it may not be a luxury to freshen their water more than once a day. Canaries kept in cages should have the bottom of their cage cleaned and recovered with pure sand once a week, preferably at a set time. The perches should be sanded clean and disinfected on a weekly basis also. These perches can well use more frequent cleanings, particularly in the spring and summer months. Drinking water and perches are often ideal breeding places for bacteria so that extra attention to their cleanliness is highly desirable. The glass or plastic around the cage should also be cleaned once a week, either with a sponge and chamois cloth or glass spray and paper towel, but in the event of the latter, we should direct the glass

Properly matched pair of Lizard canaries; cock, broken-cap Silver; hen, Gold Cap known as whole-cap.

The male with his chicks only a few days old.

Roller hen at nest. Canaries should be kept in a peaceful spot or very little will come of breeding or the rearing of the young.

spray onto the towel rather than onto the glass, for reasons that are self-evident.

Our aviaries and other types of large bird housing are also subject to weekly cleaning. The water and seed dishes should be cleaned at least every other day; the night shelter must be checked once a week for harmful insects, which, if spotted, must be exterminated. Any joints in the night shelter or the nesting boxes can be the daytime hang-out for bird lice. Take a pocket-knife and run the blade between the wood joints; if there is any sign of blood (canary blood!) on the blade, this is a sure sign that your aviary has been intruded by these pesky parasites. Spray with bird sprays available in your pet shop, and don't forget any cracks and crevices!

Our birds should have access to fresh bathing water every day, and it will be enthusiastically used by them. Naturally we do not provide bathing water outdoors during cold weather. We will touch on this subject again further in this chapter when we go into more detail regarding water.

Canaries are seed-eaters, as evidenced by their sturdy beaks. Their vegetarian diet, then, will have to possess all the elements that our canaries need: proteins, fat, carbohydrates, vitamins, calcium, and trace elements. It will probably come as no surprise that there is no seed that possesses all of these foodstuffs. This is why we use seed mixtures, which means, of course, that several different seed varieties have been used in varying quantities to form a seed mixture. There are several excellent pre-mixed seed varieties available on the market which have become world famous, and for good reason. Before we go into more detail regarding the foodstuffs, I would first point out that the value of the seed is determined by, among other factors, the amount of sunlight, humidity, and soil condition and quality from and in which the seed-bearing plant grows. I will readily admit that things are not becoming any simpler for the bird fancier at this point. We will take canary seed as an example. Scientifically known as *Phalaris canariensis*, canary seed, needless to say, will be gratefully accepted by your canaries. Although some is grown locally, most of this elongated seed, which constitutes a major part in the canary's diet, comes from Argentina, Morocco, and Australia. Three different sources immediately implies three different qualitites in form, color, and food value. The various canary seed types can be bought individually, but should then be bought on an alternating basis, this presuming of course that you mix the seed varieties yourself. As previously stated, there are very good pre-mixed brands available which offer a constant quality and ratio based on scientific tests, thus eliminating the chances we would otherwise be taking in mixing our own seeds.

As we will no doubt remember from our science studies, protein is the most important food element, since it helps to maintain and build up the bird's body. The unhatched chick starts its existence feeding upon egg white, a proteinaceous substance which is found in large quantities in a bird's egg. It would follow that an adult bird also must have protein on a daily basis. If protein is missing or given in insufficient doses, it will soon become apparent by the deteriorating condition of our canary (or other bird species for that matter). It is sure not to come as a surprise that a good, well-balanced bird menu is rich in protein. In fact, it has been determined that 12% of our canaries' daily food intake should consist of protein. We can achieve this goal by offering seed varieties that are rich in protein as their "main dish," such as canary seed, rape seed and niger seed. We will speak on the proper ratios of the various seeds a little later.

Protein consists primarily of amino acids and is an essential food element in the diet, particularly for the formation of the new protoplasm for cells, of which the body of the canary (and every living thing) is built. Protein possesses the following chemical elements: carbon, hydrogen, oxygen, nitrogen, and usually a small amount of sulphur, as well as a few other elements, depending upon the source. This summary will no doubt make it quite clear why protein is so essential for the growth, repair, and replacement of 'worn out' parts of the body. In addition to all these functions, it also generates energy through oxidation. Since protein cannot be stored by the body, it is necessary that it be available on a daily basis. If the body consumes too much protein, it will be converted into glycogen, an insoluble carbohydrate stored in the liver. Protein appears in large quantities in meat, as an example, so it is therefore a pity that canaries normally will not eat insects or their direct replacements, but of course we can offer them universal food and rearing food which contains eggs (an

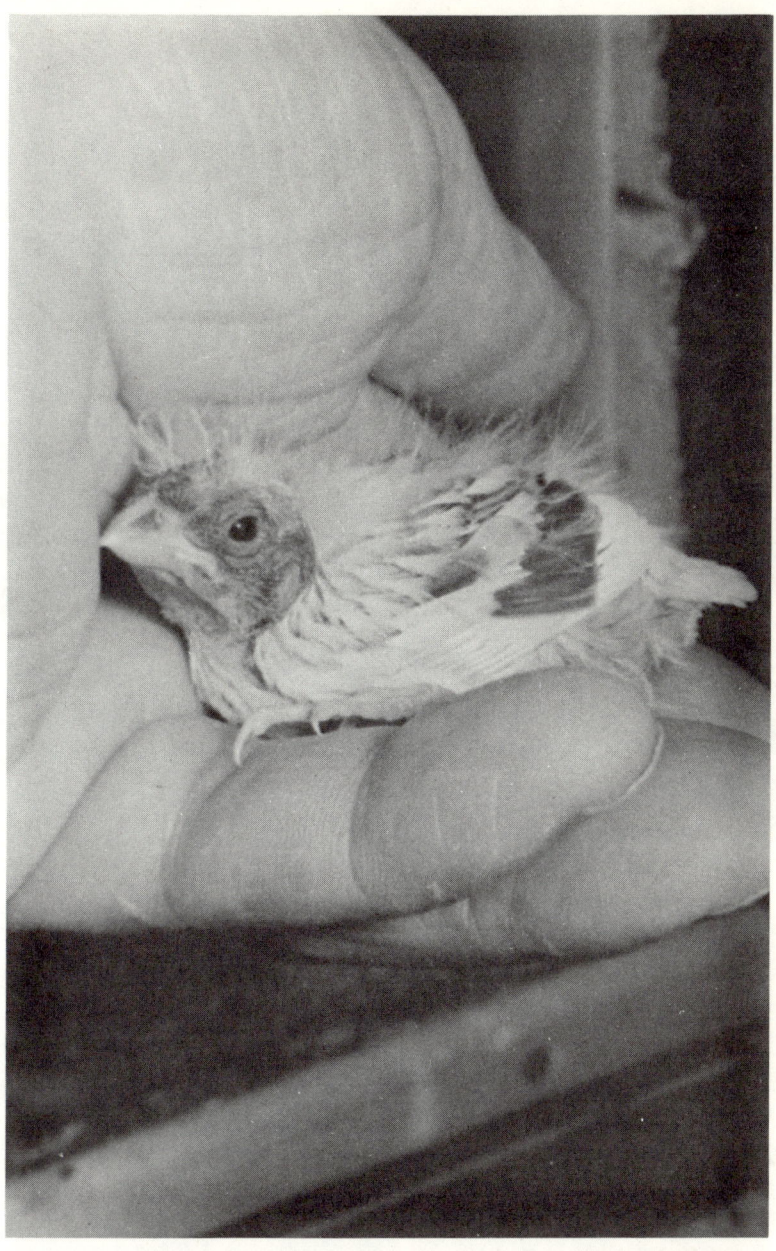

Young Roller (nestling). The chick starts its existence feeding upon egg white, a protein substance; a young chick can continue to receive protein from, among other things, bread soaked in milk.

Border Fancy chicks ready to leave the nest at three weeks of age. To receive a vitamin-rich diet as they mature canaries needs fresh seeds and greens, sprouted seeds, half-ripe weed seeds, and fruit.

animal product) instead. Milk also contains protein, and a slice of bread soaked in milk will generally be eaten by most birds. Here again, this could be substituted with rusk crumbs (sweet cookies or bread); there are even a few companies who make rusk flour (so called egg rusks) from which we can make our own chick rearing and strength foods.

Carbohydrates also play an important role in the diet. Carbohydrates contain carbon, oxygen, and hydrogen. Perhaps this does not have much meaning to you, but if I give you a few examples, I am sure you will get the picture. The following carbohydrates come to mind: glucose, $C_6H_{12}O_6$; cane sugar, $C_{12}H_{22}O_{11}$; starch $(C_6H_{10}O_5)_n$; and cellulose. For our not so chemistry-minded readers, we would point out that the formula for starch indicates that it is a fairly large molecule that consists of multiples of a $C_6H_{10}O_5$ unit. The "n" can be the equivalent of 300 and more.

You no doubt already know that carbohydrates are found in the form of starches and sugar. Carbohydrates are also found in rape seeds, which are considered to be "nut-sweet" in canary circles (and "sweet"—thus sugar—should clarify the point). Canary seeds also contain a high percentage of carbohydrates. Starch is really a form of sugar. Since sugar can be directly absorbed by the body (starch is first broken down into molecules through chemicals found in saliva), it can enter the bloodstream via the small intestine and then be transported to the tissues. At that point we could consider it as energy; in other words, as carbohydrates are burned, they supply warmth and energy. This brings us to the next fact: every gram of carbohydrates supplies 4.1 kilocalories of energy. It is no doubt interesting to know that an overabundance of carbohydrates in mammals is stored in the muscles and liver in the form of glycogen or can be converted into fat and stored under the skin. This process can be clearly observed with animals that spend a part of the year in particularly cold regions.

The function of fats is more or less the same as carbohydrates. Fats contain carbon, hydrogen, and oxygen, but of course in different ratios than carbohydrates. Among other sources, fats can be found in milk, animal fat, and egg yolks. Fat is fuel for energy and warmth, though we should keep in mind that it is considerably more difficult for the body to digest and absorb fats than carbohydrates. On the other hand, the caloric value of fat is twice as great. Impor-

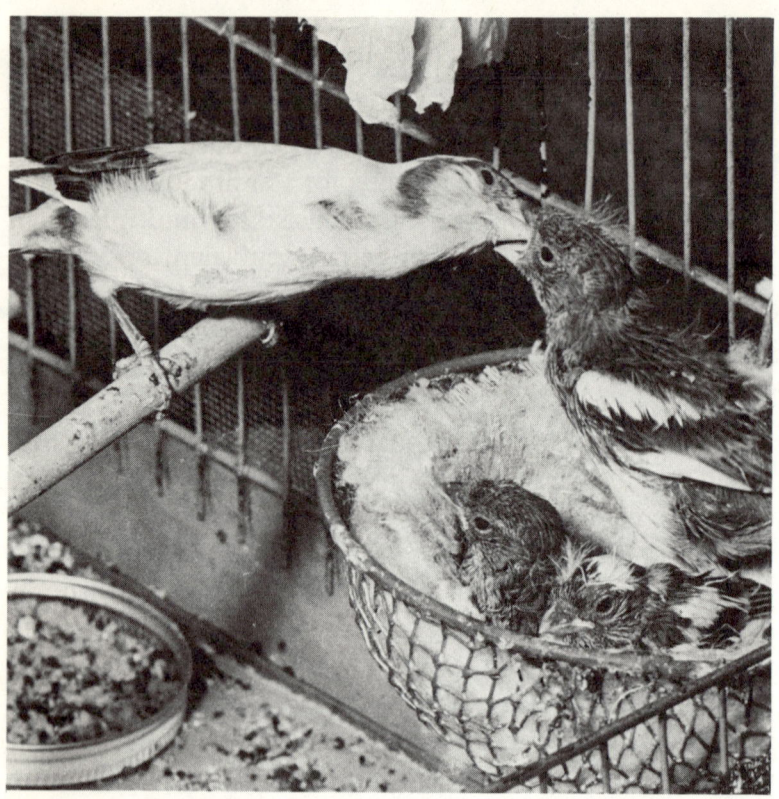

Variegated Border Fancy canary and chicks. The hen feeds the chicks with egg food rich in protein.

tant vitamins, such as A and D and the so-called "fertility vitamin," E, can be found dissolved in fats. As digestion of fat is slower than that of carbohydrates, our canaries can go much longer on fats. This certainly has its advantage in the cold seasons when the nights are long and cold and there are fewer daylight hours, which would tend to decrease the amount of food that is consumed. It is a logical conclusion that our canaries will have a greater need for seeds with a higher fat content during the fall and winter months. The following table is intended to give you some idea as to the content of the various seeds with regard to proteins, carbohydrates, and fats:

Hamburg rape seed: 14% protein, 15.8% carbohydrates, 31% fat
Linseed: 1.5% protein, 17.5% carbohydrates, 40.8% fat
Hemp: 16.2% protein, 15.8% carbohydrates, 32.5% fat
Millet: 15% protein, 60.4% carbohydrates, 5% fat
Niger seed: 17.4% protein, 17% carbohydrates, 32.5% fat
Canary seed: 13.5% protein, 50.8% carbohydrates, 5% fat
Rape seed: 19% protein, 10.4% carbohydrates, 40.2% fat

These figures should help us to make a good choice for each season.

Calcium and trace elements are found in mineral salts, of which there are a great variety. These salts and others are absolutely necessary for the chemical activities inside the

Variegated Border Fancy chicks receiving chick rearing food.

bird's body and for the building of certain tissues. As examples, the red coloring in the blood (hemoglobin) contains iron, the skeleton contains calcium, magnesium, and phosphor, and almost all cells, nerves, and body fluids cannot do without sodium and potassium. In man iodine is imperative to ensure the proper functioning of the thyroid. Besides nitrogen and sulphur in the proteins, we can also find traces of copper, cobalt, and manganese, which are also all essential. If we study calcium in a little more detail, we will all agree that calcium (particularly calcium phosphate) is tremendously important for the bird egg, which has a shell of calcium, as well as the skeleton of the chick. As far as trace elements are concerned, we need not worry about them because in normal food the salts of these elements are present, though in very small amounts, so the body can absorb and concentrate them. If we stick to a well-balanced menu, our canaries will not suffer any deficiencies of iron, potassium, magnesium, and other elements.

Then there is the subject of vitamins. Articles in bird magazines make frequent mention of the importance of offering food rich in vitamins to our feathered friends. Vitamins cause rather complicated chemical reactions which are essential to the normal metabolism processes in the broadest sense, though they have no bearing on the generation of energy. The importance of vitamins was first discovered around 1900 by Gowland, Hopkins, et al. If there is any lack of certain vitamins in our diet, the normal process of chemical reactions will be affected, with the appearance of corresponding disease symptoms as a result. Consequently, the simplest and most effective cure is to bring the diet back up to the required standards and make up for the deficiency by giving supplementary doses of the vitamin in question. If a particular vitamin(s) cannot be found in the

English type of Frilled canary, cock.

food we are giving our canaries or the amount present is too small, we will have to give vitamin preparations (obtainable in every good pet store). Usually a few drops mixed in with universal or chick rearing food will bring about a rapid improvement. Since animals—including canaries—cannot manufacture most of their own vitamins from simple elements in the manner that plants can, they will have to absorb their vitamins ready-made, through the (direct or indirect) consumption of plants.

At the moment, man has isolated over fifteen different vitamins. The most important ones to us as bird fanciers are vitamins A, B, C, D and E; there are also twelve different varieties of vitamin B. For example, the source of vitamin B_1 is wheatgerm and yeast, while B_2 is found in yeast, milk and vegetables. B vitamins are a very important group because they have an influence on the proper digestion of carbohydrates, stimulate growth, and prevent anemia. A bird can manufacture its own vitamin C if we offer it sufficient vegetables (spinach, lettuce, etc.) and some fruit or fruit substitutes, such as a few drops of orange juice mixed in with universal or chick rearing food. It is unlikely that our canaries will be deficient in the very important vitamin C providing we follow this regimen. The importance of vitamin C lies in the fact that it provides our birds with an excellent resistance to disease and effects the speedy healing of small wounds and the like.

Thanks to sunlight, vitamin D can also be formed inside the bird's body. Vitamin D can be found in cod-liver oil and egg yolks, while we should not forget to mention cream (and milk) as a source. This vitamin is also essential when one considers its importance with regard to the proper development of the skeleton; rachitis (commonly known as rickets) is the result of a deficiency in Vitamin D.

We should have been able to conclude from the above that in order to offer a menu rich in vitamins, we will have to be sure to give our birds fresh seeds, fresh greens, sprouted seeds, half-ripe weed seeds, and fruit. If our canaries are provided with the proper diet, I advise against supplementing the diet with extra vitamin preparations; the same applies to wheatgerm oil, which is sometimes served during the breeding season since it contains vitamin E and therefore is supposed to promote the fertility of the birds. Personally, I feel that wheatgerm oil need not be given to our birds as long as we offer them fresh greens and sprouted seed varieties on a daily basis. I do think it is well worthwhile to mix in with their seeds a few drops of cod-liver oil during the winter months. If we use three drops per kilo of seed, we should greatly reduce the risk of vitamin deficiencies. Of course this assumes that we give our birds sprouted seeds and greens throughout the year as well. Make sure that the seeds served are fresh, because old seeds lose a great deal of their nutritional value. This is why it is so important to obtain our seed supply from a trusted source. Never buy a seed supply to last longer than a few months, and make it a point to regularly check the purchased seeds to see if they will still germinate. Sprinkle a few seeds on a flat plate and pour a little lukewarm water on the seeds. Leave them for one day, preferably in a warm location. The second day rinse the seeds and again cover them with lukewarm water. If after four days there is still no sign of germination, we are dealing with old seeds and would be well advised to change our source of supply.

WATER

As we know, a great deal of the body of animals consists of water. Water is the essential element in the normal protoplasm in the cell, where the chemical processes take place that are so important to life. Water plays an important role in the digestion of food and in the transportation of nutrients; all chemical reactions in the body can take place only in a solution containing water. This is why water is so important in the diet. Consequently, birds must have

Couple of baby Norwich canaries. During the breeding season birds and their young should be virtually undisturbed.

access daily to pure, fresh water. If we were to study the body tissues, a biological and chemical examination of a recently deceased canary would reveal that its body is made up of over 75% water, and this is only considering the tissues! If we serve impure water, the chances of their becoming ill are great. Intestinal disorders are about the least we can expect! An ideal drinking water supply—if we could make it—would be some kind of waterfall with water streaming over rocks and a drainage gutter leading the water out of the aviary. This could be costly, but if we have a lot of birds it might be worth the effort and the difference in price over the common earthenware drinking dishes and other such items. Those dishes are open, of course, and therefore not very hygienic, not only because many birds like to take a bath in them, but because dust and other impurities find their way into them. Fountains and automatic drinkers may be subject to the same risks but to a lesser extent, because they fill up by themselves and their size is such that our canaries are not as tempted to bathe in them. If our birds stay outdoors during the winter, wire or wooden slats should be placed over the bowl because birds like to bathe no matter what the weather if given the opportunity. I do not need to elaborate on the results, such as freezing of wet feathers.

In breeding cages, fancy cages, and the like, present water in glass, porcelain or plastic containers. These are not only easy to clean, but because they are seldom very large, we will be forced to fill them with fresh water regularly. We often observe the growth of algae in water containers. This can be quite difficult to remove in closed water bottles, but if you place a few bicycle ball-bearings in the bottle while cleaning it, you will be amazed how quickly the algae disappear.

Water, then, must always be present, both in winter and the other seasons. It must be clean and will need to be replaced more often on some days than others. Regular tap

Young Border Fancies posing for one of their first photographic sessions.

water is fine, although some canary fanciers are leery of the fluoride and chlorine that are added to most water supplies. Although it has not been proved that either of these elements is damaging to our birds (they can be fatal for fish in an aquarium, but then it seems logical that water for fish must meet more strict requirements), we certainly could use rainwater filtered through a closely woven linen cloth or charcoal. This is especially recommended during the breeding season.

It is also no luxury to dissolve a few grains of iodized salt in the drinking water to supply our birds with the small amount of iodine required in their diet. Canary fanciers who have convenient access to seawater should certainly use this as drinking water for their canaries, no matter how strange it may sound. Seawater contains practically all the minerals that a canary needs, lacking only calcium. Offer seawater that is pure (a feat that is becoming more difficult with each passing day, alas) in a separate dish and replace it every day. Of course most seawater is much too salty for our birds in undiluted form (only our seabirds can consume it like that). I obtained the best results by using one teaspoon of seawater to a cup of tapwater. This same solution can be used when soaking seeds. In this manner our canaries will get all but one of the necessary minerals. Never soak more seeds than will be consumed in one day, however.

COPROPHAGY

When I stated above that calcium cannot be found in seawater, I was reminded of the canary fancier who swore up and down that canaries have no great need for calcium. In the previous pages I hope we will have proven differently. A deficiency in calcium can also cause them to start pecking at their own droppings (coprophagy) and eating them! Naturally we must immediately put a stop to this distasteful habit. First of all, we must change the seed mixture. (As you know, calcium can be found in seed.) We also try to get our birds to the point where they will gnaw at cuttlebone and grit. There are also mineral blocks available on the market which are excellent. Although it was previously thought that birds in captivity only needed minerals during the molting period, studies have definitely proved that canaries require minerals the whole year round. Should you find that your birds are not touching the cuttlebone or the mineral blocks, it would be wise to crumble them and mix them in with the seed or place them on the ground of the aviary or cage. We only do this, however, if they indicate a total lack of interest, because you will no doubt understand that gnawing on whole mineral blocks and cuttlebone has the advantage of keeping the beak in good shape.

SEEDS

In reading a few books on canaries, I was surprised by the large variety of possibilities and combinations listed and discussed under the subject of seed mixtures. Let me begin this topic by saying that most canary breeders are in agreement that their birds are better off with a simple and somewhat plain menu than with one which is quite varied. Providing we keep the essential requirements in mind, however, we cannot condemn a varied menu. We should not, of course, give our birds all kinds of goodies, such as lumps of sugar and pieces of cookies.

For those who keep a canary in a cage indoors, I feel that the most sensible and economical way to feed the bird is to buy a good brand of pre-mixed seed. Remember to seal the box properly when putting it back in the closet; this will also keep the dust out. Canaries in an aviary need a fairly large assortment of seeds. This should be understandable because of the fact that they spend the entire day flying around outdoors in the (hopefully) fresh air . . . and outdoor air makes one hungrier! The canary in the indoor cage cannot enjoy all this, but of course he does not use as much energy either. Caged canaries are generally not bred, since someone interested in keeping a canary in a cage usually just wants a good singer, so they have different food requirements.

The same basic needs, however, apply to both the aviary canary and the canary placed in a breeding cage. In both cases, the following menu seems to be the best, and I would add that some twenty years of experience are behind this combination. Each seed is followed by the ratio figure.

1) Canary seed (so called Moroccan canary seed): 35

The last egg the hen lays can be recognized by its darker color. Eggs usually number from three to as many as six.

2) Rape seed (so called nut-sweet summer seed): 30
3) Hamburger rape seed: 10
4) Niger seed: 8
5) Groats: 8
6) Hemp: 2
7) Maw seed: 2
8) Lettuce seed: 2
9) Linseed: 1
10) Plantain seed: 2

A canary kept in an indoor cage can be given a mixture of canary seed, rape seed, and Hamburg rape seed in a ratio of 5-70-25. I would repeat, however, that I advise against mixing your own seed for a canary in a cage; it will end up costing more in the long run. In addition to the mentioned mix, add some treat mix consisting of canary seed, hulled oats, white lettuce seed, niger seed, and maw seed in the following ratio: 50-25-5-15-5. This mix is readily available in your pet store, although of course we could mix it ourselves. Finally we can add a small amount of hemp, plantain seed, and linseed to the above concoction. Song canaries such as the Harz canaries should be kept primarily on the latter mixture. It will have quite an effect on their song. I would also like to interject an additional note to song canary breeders at this point: if you feel your canaries are singing too softly, you should increase the percentage of the treat mix offered and temporarily cut out universal food, strength food, and white bread soaked in milk. Apart from the seeds described above, canaries must have access to a rich variety of weed seeds. As a matter of fact, they will not only eat the seeds but often the greens as well.

WEEDS

Although wild birds will instinctively not eat poisonous plants such as the black nightshade, belladonna, lily of the valley, and thimbleweeds, this is not necessarily the case with birds that have been domesticated for centuries. Fur-

An eighteen-day-old chick. The switch from egg food to regular canary seed mixtures must be gradual for young birds.

ther studies, however, have yet to be made on this subject. The assumption that canaries, budgerigars, and zebra finches will avoid all poisonous weeds is still in question. Therefore, it would seem logical to take the safe route and only make available those plants which we can definitely identify. It would be advisable to have a simple guidebook on hand to assist in making these identifications, preferably one with clear illustrations. *Weeds, a Golden Nature Guide* published by Western Publishing Co., is a small and inexpensive book that will make child's play out of identifying common yard and field plants. Several other titles should be available at your local bookstore.

A word of warning with regard to searching for weeds: as you know, insecticides are widely used in orchards, along highways, on land used for agriculture, etc. Plants that have been sprayed with an insecticide are extremely dangerous to the health of our birds. When looking for weeds, be sure you can see enough insects flying about. If everything is too quiet, it would be wise to find a different location for your weed source. Of course most of us will probably have no shortage of weeds right in our own garden! Perhaps even our window flower boxes might produce a few. In this event we can really be sure that they have not been sprayed. If we store weed seeds in a dry, cool place, we can even give them to our birds during the winter months.

The following plants would be suitable:

Hedge nettle (*Stachys arvensis*). The stalk of this plant either lies down or stands upright. The plant itself is lightly covered with 'hair.' It has pale pink flowers and grows in profusion on sandy and limy soil from the month of May to late into the fall. Height: 15-25 cm.

Canada thistle (*Cirsium arvense*). This is a flowering plant with a straight stalk. The leaves are lancet-shaped, deeply indented, and have prickly teeth. Flowers are lilac to reddish purple in color. This weed is very common along the banks of creeks and rivers, on grassy plains, and on land that lies fallow. Flowers bloom from June through September. Height: about 60 cm.

Perennial sow thistle (*Sonchus arvensis*). If we snap this weed we can see the white milky sap. The leaves are heart-shaped, deeply indented, encircle the stem, and have prickly teeth. Many glandular hairs are found on the stalk. It is commonly found in fields, farm land, and sometimes fallow land. It blooms from July to deep into the fall. Height 60-150 cm.

Rabbitsfood grass (*Polypogon monspeliensis*). This plant has a straight stalk and a somewhat rough sheath. It is commonly found almost everywhere, particularly along the

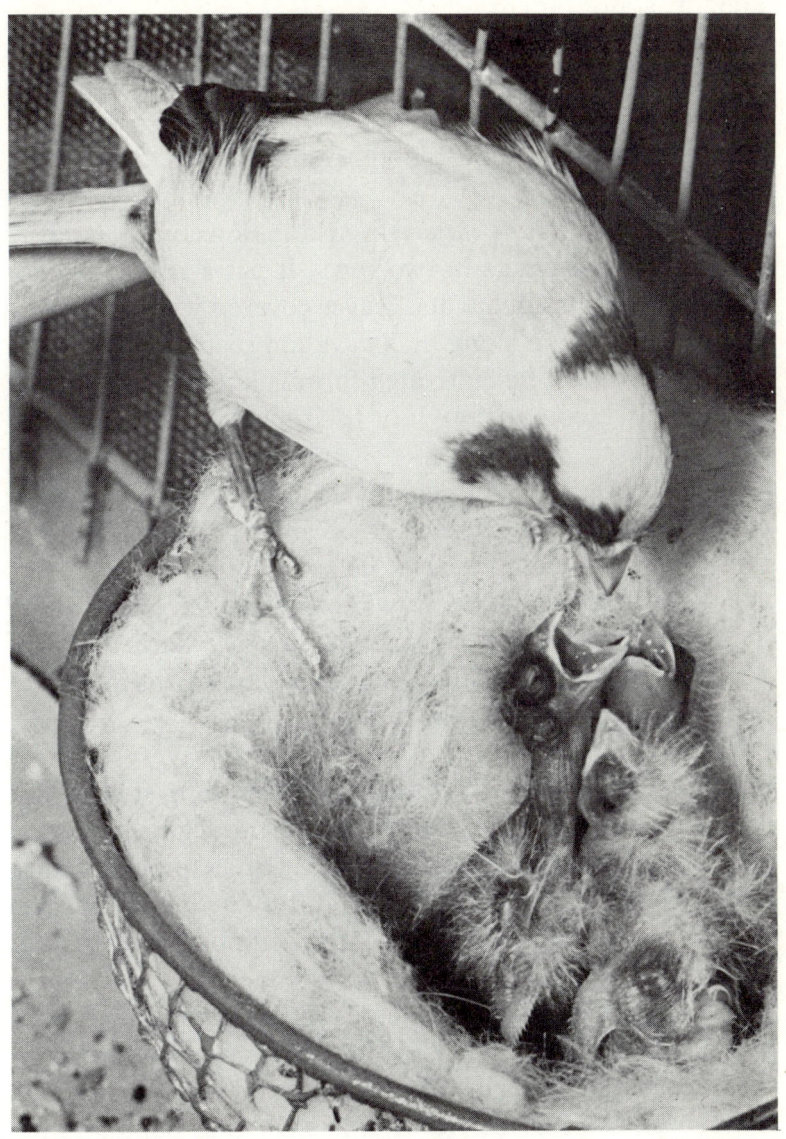

For the first few days the young chicks should be fed egg food.

shoulders of highways. It blooms from June to September. Height: about 60 cm.

Mugwort (*Artemisia vulgaris*). A somewhat shrubby plant. Flower spikes upright and are grouped in bunches. Yellow composite flowers. These plants are very common along highways. They bloom from July to September. Height: 60-120 cm.

Chicory (*Cichoram intybus*). A blue-flowered composite with involucral bracts in two rows. It has a straight-standing stalk, with branches and leaves covered with stiff hairs. It is quite common along highways and roads and along the banks of rivers. The cultivated form is known as *Cichoram sativum*. It blooms from July to August. Height: 30-120 cm.

Spanish needles, sticktights (various species of the genus *Bidens*). The leaves are dark green and usually made up of three parts, sometimes five. Heart of flower is brown-yellow. These plants are very common, particularly along the water's edge and in marshy areas, where a lot of nitrogen is present in the soil. They bloom from July to September. Height: to 90 cm.

Yarrow (*Archillea millefolium*). This is a very suitable plant for our purposes. It has straight-standing stems. The leaves are twice to three times pinnate, the segments linear-lanceolate, spreading. White or sometimes pinkish white small flowers bloom from June to October. It is very common along highways and in fact, almost everywhere. Height: 15-45 cm.

Snowball, high-bush cranberry (*Viburnum opulus*). Looking much like a honeysuckle at first glance, this quite large shrub has large-toothed, soft, three-lobed leaves (sometimes five lobes). It bears berries that are not that popular with the birds. The flowers are white. Perimeter flowers are big

Border Fancy hen feeding young with high protein egg food.

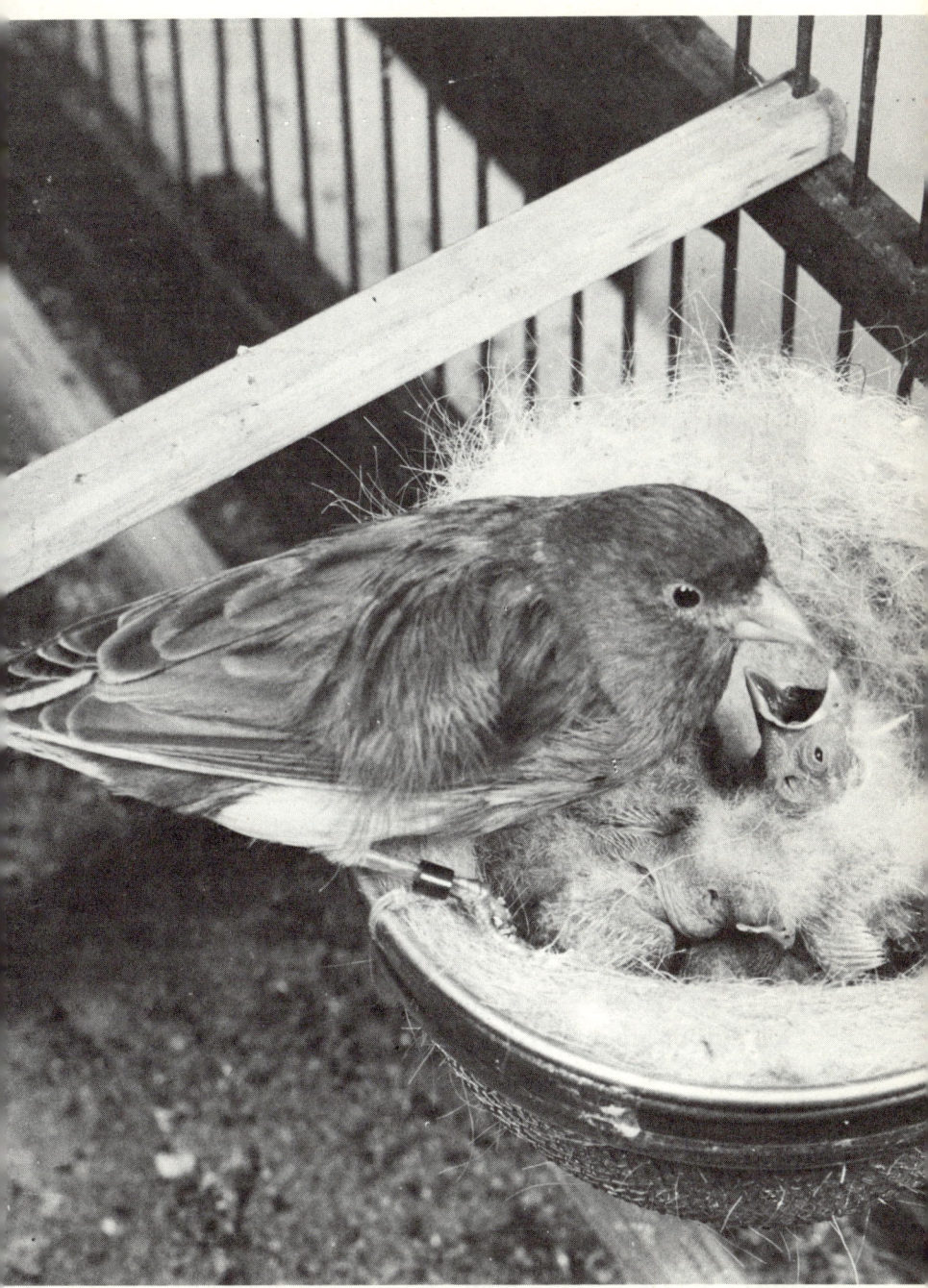

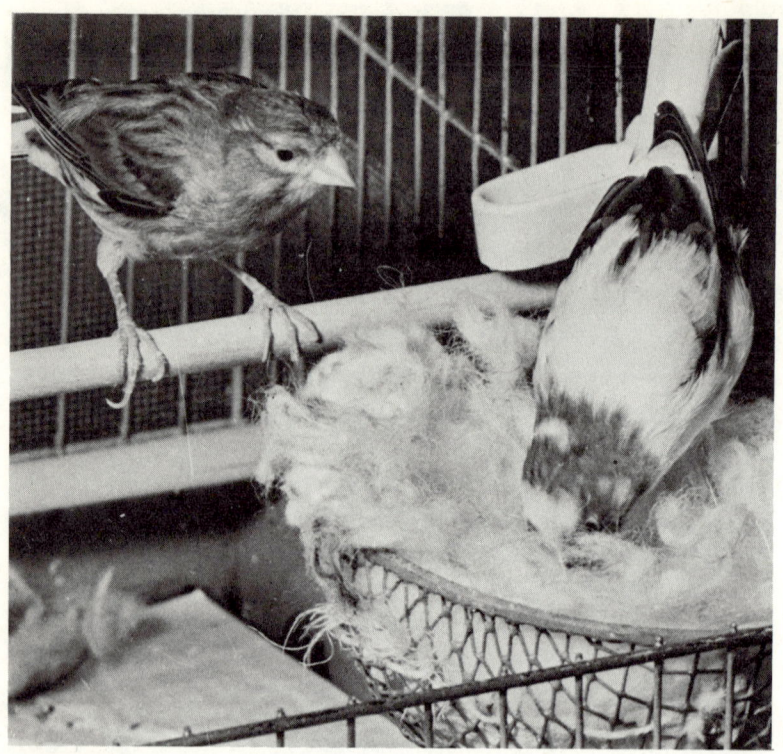

Pair of Border Fancy canaries constructing a nest.

and serve as bait for insects. This plant is common in wooded areas, both moist and dry, in dunes, etc. It blooms from May to June. Height: 150-300 cm.

Goldenrods (various species of the genus *Solidago*). These plants have a thin stalk with finely toothed elongated leaves. There are delicate yellow flowers in bunches. Goldenrods are quite common in forests of deciduous trees, on sandy soil, and on slopes. Flowers bloom from July to October. Height: 15-90 cm.

Meadow salsify (*Tragopogon pratensis*). This leafy straight-standing stalk has long, grass-like leaves. It is noteworthy that the yellow flowers are only open when the sun is shining and close again during the afternoon. The plant is very common along highways and other grassy areas. It blooms from May to August. Height: 25-60 cm.

Hemp nettle (*Galeopsis tetrahit*). The stalk is straight-standing with leaves that are oval to elongated and covered with soft hair. The white to purple-red flowers have a red marking on the lower lip. Common on cultivated land and along roads, this plant blooms from June to October. Height: 15-75 cm.

Wild mustard (*Brassica arvensis*). This plant bearing small yellow flowers is related to, among others, rape seed. It has smooth black seeds and blooms from May to September. It is common on cultivated land and along highways. Height: 30-80 cm.

Falseflax (*Camelina sativa*). The straight-standing stalk has some branching at the top and has leaves that can be either toothed or smooth-edged. The lower leaves are lancet-shaped. There are round or pear-shaped fruits. It has small yellow flowers and oil-containing seeds. It is very common on cultivated land and blooms from May to July. Height: 95 cm.

Nesting material may be purchased in pet shops in handy-packed, sterilized bundles.

Clear yellow Border Fancy.

Knapweed (*Centaurea jacea*). This plant has a straight stalk with irregular branching. The leaves are either broadly egg-shaped or lancet-shaped, the upper leaves often somewhat oblanceoalte, sessile, and with one or two large teeth. Common along highways, in dry fields, etc., it blooms from July into the fall. Height: to 75 cm.

Common groundsel (*Senecio vulgaris*). Recognized by the elongated clusters of yellow flowers and deeply lobed leaves. It is extremely common almost everywhere and practically the whole year around. Height: 10-50 cm.

Common chickweed (*Stellaria media*). There are several varieties. The stalk has one or sometimes two rows of hair. The leaves are egg-shaped with rather short stems depending upon the variety. The small white flowers have three to ten stamens and petals of the same length as the calyx. Chickweed can be found almost the whole year. This is the ideal green food for practically all our birds, in addition to canaries.

Stitchwort (*Stellaria graminea*). The soft stalk, which can be either standing up or lying down, has small white flowers. It is common along highways, on cultivated land, and in moist soil. The stem and leaves are a grass-green color. Blooms from May to July. Height: to 45 cm.

Dock or sorrel (*Rumex obtusifolius*). This plant has a tall straight-standing stalk with small pointy leaves at the upper part of the stalk and egg-shaped or heart-shaped leaves at the lower part. It is common practically everywhere and blooms from June to October. Height: 90-150 cm. The species *Rumex acetosa*, common sorrel, is probably the most suitable of all the dock species. This species has arrow-shaped leaves and some reddish fuzz on the fruit. Covering of nutlet rounded-cordate with tiny round swelling. It is very common and sometimes cultivated as a vegetable. Height to 100 cm.

Kentucky blue grass (*Poa pratensis*). We particularly recommend this plant for aviary use. It has long runners. It

is very common even in very dry areas and blooms from May to June. Height: about 60 cm.

Spear grass (*Poa annua*). This plant is very common as a weed of farms and gardens almost everywhere. It blooms almost the whole year around. Height: 15-30 cm.

Plantains (family Plantaginaceae) have basal rosette of large leaves and small greenish flowers in spikes. Broadleaf plantain (*Plantago major*) is used a great deal. The leaves are weakly covered with hair or smooth. The leaves are attached by long stems. The dense, narrow spike of small yellowish white flowers has anthers that are first a purple shade and later turn white. It blooms from May into the fall and is very common practically everywhere. Height: to 45 cm. Buckhorn plantain (*Plantago lanceolata*) has a thick root with many runners. The oval or lancet-shaped leaves are quite pointy. It has yellowish anthers, is very common, and blooms from April to late into the fall. Height: to 45 cm. *Plantago media* has leaves attached to short stems and with a dense covering of hair. The anthers are lilac. It is common along rivers and on lime-rich soil, but can also be found along highways. It blooms from May to August. *Plantago coronopus* has leaves arranged in a basal rosette; they are generally deeply indented. The anthers are yellowish white. This plant is particulalry common along the seashore and blooms from May to October.

Needless to say, there are many more weeds that could be suitable as "greens" or for their seeds. I would like to stress the fact that in order to hope for successful breeding results, weed and grass seeds are an absolute must. Keep in mind, however, that towns and many farmers do a great deal of spraying with insecticides. Any insecticide is dangerous to our birds, so keep your wits about you!

Border Fancy canaries; young and cock (in the middle).

SPROUTED SEED

Sprouted seeds are always welcome, but especially just before and during the breeding period. It is best to use rape seed or niger seed, or you could purchase the special assortment of sprouted seed mixes available at any good seed supply store. Use a smooth, not too thin cloth and moisten it with lukewarm water. Spread the cloth out on a flat plate or a cookie sheet. Sprinkle the seeds onto the cloth and place the whole thing in a warm, humid location. When the seeds burst open, rinse them off with a little water, using a strainer, and serve them to canaries in a separate dish. Do not give more than your birds can consume in one day, and throw out whatever is left at night. Seed that has gone sour will only cause problems such as intestinal upsets. Weed seeds can be used in the above manner, too. Further, it does not take a great deal of effort to plant some weed seeds on the soil floor of the aviary; sprouting seeds and seedlings

Only minutes old, the newly born chick is almost bare of feathers.

Border Fancy.

are much enjoyed by your birds. In fact, you need not remove seed that the birds have spilled from the feeder; these may develop into a little green corner where your birds will gratefully "nose around" looking for seedings.

CHICK REARING AND STRENGTH FOODS

Chick rearing food is actually a kind of egg food. It can be bought under several different names which enjoy world renown and can, of course, be directly offered to your birds. Chick rearing food, as the name implies, is essential during the breeding period. It often happens that breeders switch to a different brand, particularly in the breeding season, because they feel that their mediocre results of the previous season(s) were due to the brand they were then using. Usually, however, there are other reasons for unsuccessful clutches. Keep in mind that every brand available has a great deal of research behind it and that competition is much too fierce to give an inferior brand much of a chance to survive. If you still feel that you will have better results with a different brand than the one you are currently using (perhaps because at a club meeting you heard someone bragging about the fantastic results he achieved using a particular brand of food), then of course go ahead and change brands. Never do this, however, during the breeding season; allow ample time before the breeding season starts so that your birds have the opportunity to become accustomed to their new food. Don't go adding all kinds of vitamins to these prepared foods, as an overdose usually results in your birds becoming sick. Among our older canary breeders there are probably many who do not want any part of these prepared foods, preferring to make their own concoction of one hard-boiled egg and four rusks. I must admit that personal experience has shown that this mixture achieved very good results. Boil the egg for ten minutes, and of course use only fresh eggs. If you feel so inclined, you could add a little lettuce and some maw seed as well as a little grated carrot and finely chopped chickweed. Do not use egg powder, as this can very easily cause constipation. It should go without saying that this concoction, too, must be made fresh daily.

I am sure you will understand that young, recently flown-out birds must also have access to this egg food. Their switch over to regular canary seed mixtures must be gradual. Incidentally, it is no luxury to also offer canaries in a cage some chick rearing food from time to time. Their health can only benefit from this.

Canaries should also be given some "strength foods" on a daily basis, though care should be taken that they do not

Variegated Border Fancy.

overfeed themselves on this type of food. A good guide would be one teaspoon per day per canary. It is unlikely, anyway, that they would eat more than this if given the opportunity. Should they go overboard with it some time, it's still not the end of the world! Canaries kept in cages can empty a treat dish every other day.

Strength food is available in prepared form, but for those who prefer to make their own, here is a recipe: 4 parts canary seed, 3 parts maw seed, 5 parts hulled oats, 1 part hemp, 1 part linseed, 1 part niger seed, 1 part lettuce seed, and 1 part millet spray or a different kind of panicum millet. I should point out that lettuce seed is quite expensive; we could leave it out and substitute sweet summer rape seed, which song canaries can't get enough of; in fact, it is the main food for Harz canaries and Waterslagers.

It is important to reduce the amount of hemp in the strength food a few weeks before a show, since it often causes the plumage of our color canaries to become a little less vivid. Those canary owners who are interested in claiming top prizes in local, national, or international shows should not offer hemp to their birds! Instead of hemp, it is better to give them cracked sunflower seeds, which will do much to improve the shine of the birds' plumage.

GREENS

Greens must never be left out of a bird's menu. The importance of greens was emphasized when I discussed weeds. A canary in a cage should also be given some greens. At least once a week, and preferably twice, a canary in a cage should be offered a lettuce leaf, some spinach, cabbage, endives, a piece of carrot, or chickweeds. The ideal, of course, would be to offer a small amount of greens on a daily basis. The greens must be fresh, and any left over should be removed toward the end of the day before your canary goes to sleep. To ensure that we are offering safe, unsprayed vegetables, we could cultivate our own if we enjoy this sort of thing. If you do, I suggest you choose to grow spinach or endives.

FRUIT

Many canaries love fruit, such as pieces of apple, pear, tomato, pineapple, melon, cherries, grapes, grapefruit and berries. Large pieces are best stuck onto a nail that has been hammered into a piece of wood so that the fruit won't become filthy on the aviary floor. We can also place pieces in special wire fruit holders. Their practicality seems somewhat obscure to me, though, since the fruit ends up falling through the wire sooner or later anyway.

MINERALS

With a good menu it is unlikely that your birds will suffer from any mineral deficiencies. There are several mineral preparations that can be purchased, however. If our birds get enough minerals, late molt, egg binding, and other such discomforts will be rare. These prepared minerals need only be sprinkled on the floor of the aviary or cage, so it certainly does not require much effort. In this regard, we would point out that when we use special bird charcoal it is best to place this in a separate little dish rather than on the floor, especially when served in an aviary or breeding cage. Charcoal is extremely helpful to the chemical reactions that take place within our little feathered friends, but I suppose you have gathered that already!

GRIT AND CUTTLEBONE

Grit and cuttlebone are essential. Grit is a big help to the digestive system (the grinding of seeds in the crop), and cuttlebone assists with the formation of calcium. Cuttlebone can be bought in the store, complete with holder, and is very reasonably priced. If you should have access to unprepared (natural) cuttlebone, be sure to soak them for a few days first, because their salt content is too high for direct consumption by our canaries. Cuttlebone is also very important during molting. It would be a good idea to always have some on hand so that our birds need never do without.

LARD

During the winter, our canaries can well use a little extra fat. This is why some people occasionally hang a piece of bacon rind or a little lard in the cage or aviary or even (surprise, surprise!) a soupbone attached to a wire and hung up against the bars or wire. The birds enjoy pecking at it, and it can only be good for their health.

A blue variegated white Yorkshire.

4: A LITTLE ORNITHOLOGY

Ornithology is the study of birds in the broadest sense of the word. Many an aviculturist could well call himself an ornithologist if he studies his birds with regard to their behavior, the way in which they build their nests, rear their young, etc. Although he is only studying a small part of this branch of zoology, he is still concerning himself with the observation, record keeping, and study of the birds in his care. The professional ornithologist goes a step further and may involve himself, as an example, with the study of the structure of the various bird species; he digs deeply into the physiology, life-style and behavior, classification, and distribution of birds in an attempt to come up with new and/or further information. It would not be too presumptuous to conclude that even prehistoric man studied birds, judging from the cave drawings dating back to that era. In any event, we can learn from the Bible that there have always been people who have involved themselves with the study of birds. Among the works of Aristotle (384-322 B.C.) there was a classification of birds. Because there are so many genera with countless representatives (over 8,500 species) and because birds can be recognized quite readily, many scholars and fanciers alike have become experts in the field of ornithology. Birds are studied by such a great number of people not only because of a kind of magnetism people feel toward birds because of their lovely colors or their interesting behavior during the breeding period or during migrations, but also for purely practical reasons, such as their economic importance (food) or because they offer excellent assistance in the extermination of harmful insects. Therefore, it should not be considered too out of place to include a small chapter on ornithology, giving us a little insight into exactly what a bird looks like, much of which is of course also applicable to the canary.

GENERAL TRADEMARKS

Birds belong to the great Vertebrata division (subphylum of phylum Chordata) of the animal kingdom. They are warm-blooded (or homoiothermic) and their upper limbs have been formed into wings. An important point is that birds are immediately recognizable by the feathers that cover their skin. Other characteristics are that practically all birds can fly and that they lay eggs as part of their reproductive cycle. The front of their skull has been elongated to form a beak or bill, of which the upper mandible cannot be moved; exceptions to this rule, among others, are the parrots, parrakeets, and birds of prey, which can open and close their upper mandible.

In reality, the feathers are the only visible trademark that sets our feathered friends apart from the rest of the vertebrate animals. As mentioned earlier, the feathers are formed by the skin. The skin itself is very loosely fitted around the body and is very dry, since there are no sweat glands. When a bird is feeling rather warm it sits with its beak open. The feathers form a beautiful insulating layer covering the entire body except for the legs and feet (there are some exceptions to this rule too) and help maintain a constant body temperature and act as a water repellent (think of geese and ducks for example). The wings are very well developed and serve as a flight instrument for most birds; some can even use them very successfully when fighting—and when we say "fighting" we mean two birds giving each other some sound hits with their wings! The wings generally cover a surprisingly large area and are extremely light in weight.

Feather characteristics, known as buff (coarse) and yellow (fine), have nothing to do with color, but are used to indicate two forms of feather structure.

FEATHERS

When we take a look at a feather, for example one of the flight feathers of the wing, we see a kind of coil of loose down attached to it where it becomes the quill, the quill itself having a 'flag' both to the right and left. The flag consists of barbules held together by small hooklets, which indeed are hooks that fit exactly into an indentation of the barbule in front. The advantage of this piece of engineering is that whenever the feather becomes a little ruffled or damaged through flying or other causes, the bird can straighten it out with the help of his beak.

All flight feathers are attached to muscles which can alter the angle of the feathers. This can be clearly seen when a bird which is ill sits shivering with puffed up feathers in the corner of cage or aviary. Feathers also have a nerve con-

Feather structure (buff). Canaries' feather structure is one of the factors that give most varieties their pleasing sleek appearance.

nection which can cause a prickling effect when the feathers are touched; we could compare this to the whiskers of a cat.

The down feathers are very soft and, since they are located close to the body, serve to hold the warm air near the bird. In contrast, the flight feathers and coverts are broad and flat and give a bird its shape, which is usually something like a torpedo. These larger feathers also serve to give some protection against the penetration of air flow. As previously mentioned, the feathers give the bird a streamlined shape during flight and the entire build of the skeleton accentuates this as well.

As we know, the legs and toes are covered with scales, a leftover from their forebears, the reptiles. These scales fit one over the other. Another remarkable feature is their so-called 'third eyelid,' a transparent disc known scientifically as the nictitating membrane, which moves straight across the eye. This eyelid can be clearly observed with dozing or just awakened birds.

FLYING

Why is a bird so well suited for flying? The first reason, of course, is the upper limbs modified as wings and covering a large area thanks to the feathers. The second reason, I would say, is the large breast muscles which take care of the pulling down of the wings. In many species these large breast muscles often weigh more than one-fifth of the bird's total weight. Next I would draw your attention to the breastbone to which these muscles are attached. The extremely well developed coracoid bones (from New Latin coracoides "bone shaped like a crow's beak") are also well worth mentioning because these transfer the propelling power of the wings to the body. Noteworthy, too, is the sturdy, stiff skeleton which serves as a framework to which the flight muscles are attached. As an example, the posterior vertebrae have been fused together and cannot be

Border Fancy cock feeding the female at the onset of mating.

moved separately, which is not the case among other vertebrates, including mammals. The bones of the skeleton are hollow, greatly reducing the weight of the bird and therefore also contributing to flight efficiency. Finally the "wind bags," which we will discuss in more detail a little later, are also important.

PROPULSION

Although not all bird species use the same manner of propulsion in flight, it is safe to say that birds in general can execute an active flight, which we understand to be a "thrust and row" flight, and a passive "sailing and gliding" flight. Many bird species, incidentally, use these types of propulsion in various ways.

What do we mean by active flight? The word "active" implies that the movement is not entirely involuntary, but that the bird itself is doing something. With a thrusting flight the bird pulls his breast muscles together, causing the wings to go down. We probably remember from our natural science classes that the resistance of the air against the stretched out wing causes the upward propulsion. This propulsion is transferred through the coracoid bones to the sternum and continues through the center of gravity of the bird, causing the entire bird to become airborne. According to MacKean, "In addition to the upward thrust, there is also a forward propulsion generated through the flipping down of the primaries at the time that the wings are brought down, which then works as a propeller, particularly at the upper part of the wing. When the wings are thrust down, the forward edge of the wing lies lower than the back edge, causing the air to be pushed backward and the bird therefore is pushed forward. Speaking in general terms, we can say that the secondaries are involved in the upward motion, while the primaries are greatly responsible for the forward motion."

MacKean continues: "The alula* can be important when a bird takes off, because it can generate some forward propulsion; during flight it can maintain an even airstream above the wing area. The upward thrust of the wings is executed faster than the downward thrust. A smaller chest muscle contracts to bring the wings upward, since the tendon runs through an opening in the shoulder to the upper part of the upper arm bone. Quite often the arm is only turned a little, so that the front is higher than the back edge and the air stream lifts the bird upwards. The wing is bent at the wrist during the upward thrust, thereby reducing the amount of resistance. In addition, the manner in which the primaries and secondaries are designed, one overlapping the other like

* Group of small feathers at the bend of the wing.

Border Fancies; two green adults (above-left; below-right), and three ten-week-old youngsters.

Two Border Fancy canaries; the one on the right is self-green.

tiles on a roof, causes a maximum of resistance during the downward thrust and a minimum during the upward thrust.

"With the gliding flight, the wings are stretched out and used as a sail, causing the bird to glide downward along the 'air cushion,' losing altitude and gaining a forward momentum. Sometimes rising warmer air streams (thermics) or gusts of wind can be used to gain altitude (sailing flight) without the use of wing motions, such as is done by seagulls and buzzards. In general, swift flying birds have a small wing surface area and a large wing span with particularly well developed primaries, while slower birds have shorter, broader wings with well developed secondaries."

From these somewhat technical notations we can conclude that the speed of flight can vary a great deal from species to species. A very fast flier is no doubt the swift (*Apus apus*), which can attain a speed of some 160 kilometers (approximately 99 miles) per hour! A carrier pigeon, on the other hand, takes a little easier, doing about 60 (approximately 37 miles) k.p.h.!

Of course it is understandable that the tail feathers help to stabilize the flying bird, while they also perform an excellent function during braking and landing.

With regard to walking, because of the posture of a bird the center of gravity falls under the joint of the thigh bone and pelvis, which is particularly obvious when observing the walk (more like a waddle!) of ducks and other waterfowl.

RESPIRATION

Every bird, be it an ostrich or a canary, has relatively small lungs which differ in a number of factors from those of man and other mammals. They are not elastic, for starters, and do not have any small air pockets; in place of these we find countless branches which eventually unite in air passages. These are virtually encircled with hair follicles. The lungs are attached at the back side of the chest cavity.

Before air enters the lungs it is first inhaled, of course, and comes through the windpipe or trachea. This is a long tube held open by rings of cartilage. It runs from the beak to the body cavity where, just as in man, it splits into two short branches, bronchi, each of which empties into the lungs. The bronchus in turn splits into many progressively smaller tubes which pierce through the lung tissue and empty into the air sacs as tubes. These air sacs have extremely thin walls and fit exactly into the cavity; or, to put it a better way, they precisely fill the cavity between the organs and the muscles located there. Most species possess ten air sacs—five pairs. The air sacs located toward the back are generally the largest.

We already know that the breast bone (or sternum) is pulled upward when a bird is on the wing; this results, of course, in the natural consequence that the internal space is considerably reduced with the pulling together of the chest muscles. Through this decrease in size it follows that the air sacs are pushed in a little, so that air is pushed out from the wind pipes of the lungs to the bronchi, from there to the trachea, and out through the nostrils. The chest muscles will see to it that the body cavity resumes its normal size during relaxation, so that air can again be sucked into the air sacs through the bronchi.

There are only a relatively small number of blood vessels present in the air sacs so, understandably, only little absorption of oxygen is realized; on the other hand, when the oxygen arrives in the lungs through the small tubes, the many hair follicles absorb oxygen in their walls and expel carbonic acid. I would like to quote MacKean once again, who said this was a very efficient manner in which to obtain oxygen and expel carbonic acid because "there is no 'dead space'; fresh air is rapidly transported throughout the lungs and exchange takes place twice, both on the way in and the way out. Because the most powerful flight movements also compress the air sacs the most, the increased intake of oxygen fulfills the increased need of the active muscles and speeds up the removal of carbonic acid. When a bird is not in flight, the ribs are moved by muscles which squeeze the body cavity and release again, thereby forcing air in and out of the windbags. Under normal circumstances the muscles are actively involved with exhalation, while with mammals it is the inhalation that is caused by the pulling together of the muscles."

MacKean in his well documented book *Introduction to Biology*, from which much of this chapter was gleaned, purposely gives a fairly simplified explanation on the respira-

The Norwich canary is known as "bull-necked" because of its short, thick neck.

tion of birds; many secondary details have not been mentioned. By his own admission, he does not go more deeply into the details, such as the fact that the oxygen that makes its way into the air sacs in the back part of the body through a rather complicated passage (namely through the lungs to the air sacs located in the front of the bird's body) is expelled through the nostrils, with a great many "valves" preventing the back-flow of the air. It is also interesting to point out the ability that many diving water birds have, namely that of sending the oxygen back and forth several times from one pair of wind bags to the next until most of the oxygen has been absorbed by the lungs.

5: KEEPING CANARIES

The best time to start keeping canaries is during the months of November and December, because the breeding period is then behind us and our birds, if they have been well cared for, will have finished molting and will be donning their true plumage in full color and correct markings; the singers among them will be "in song"; and, last but not least, the breeder will have had a chance to carefully select the stock he is offering for sale. On this last point I am assuming that your source is a reputable breeder who will only come "on the market" with quality stock.

Buying birds is largely a matter of trust anyway. Because it is not at all uncommon to have birds offered for sale that are not in the best of shape, it seems essential to me that a beginning bird enthusiast should take an experienced aviculturist along with him. Naturally it is very important that, once you decide to start with this enchanting hobby, you obtain the best quality birds available. The more beautiful the bird, the more beautiful the offspring! This last comment, however, does not mean to imply that we should only be concerned with outer appearances; a canary that earns a great many points at a show is not necessarily a good breeder. This is why it is always a good idea to ask for details regarding a bird's ancestry; every good canary breeder keeps adequate records so that checking into a bird's family tree should not cause any problems. This will often reveal enough to help you decide one way or the other.

WHAT DOES A GOOD CANARY LOOK LIKE?

The first impression you should get from a bird that you may consider buying is one of liveliness. It should not be

Border Fancy (blue).

lethargic, but quick in movement. It should have a good build, though it is quite alright if it is on the sturdy side; the neck, back, and tail must form one line. The chest should be broad and the breastbone should not stick out. When we check this part of the bird's body with our fingers it should not feel "sharp" or small. Blow the feathers out of the way and check to make sure that the chest area is not reddish blue in color. Check the vent area, which should be clean and devoid of any sticky, dirty feathers. The stomach should also be subject to our inspection; under no circumstances should the intestines be visible through the skin (they show up as dark coils in lesser quality birds). When we hold the canary in the palm of our hand it should not shiver excessively, since this is definitely not just a matter of nerves but would indicate that the bird is weak and very likely ill, perhaps with a cold or intestinal upset. Blue,

Border Fancy (green).

puffed up stomachs, moisture coming through the nostrils, and damaged feet, eyes, wings or head all point to a lesser quality bird. All canaries, with the exception of the pied variety, have 12-14 tail quills, and if we spread the wing between thumb and forefinger it will become readily clear to us if the bird has lost any major wing feathers. The general appearance of our bird's plumage should be smooth and compact, unless we are dealing with frilled canaries.

THE SELECTION

Many fanciers, and certainly not just beginners, buy some birds here and there and barely look at what they buy! Or they just take a good look at the canary (let's stick to color canaries for the time being) and do not bother to ask about the ancestry of the male. It seems that a great many breeders are not aware that while the female only transmits

Gloster Fancy Corona (crested).

the coloring that she shows, the male can possess several hidden characteristics that may reveal themselves through the offspring. Color canary breeders, therefore, need to inquire about the forebears of the male that they are considering; otherwise they may be in for some unpleasant surprises when the young start to show their plumage. With song canaries the case is even more complicated, because not only can a cock that is a good singer come from parents who are not, but the female must be the offspring of a good pair of parents that must both be of the same "song type." Particular song breeds such as the Harz and Waterslagers should be bought from a reputable breeder if one wishes to develop competition birds that deserve that title within about three to five years.

Of course, color canaries should also be purchased from a trusted source, a place where we can be sure that breeding does not take place to irresponsible degrees of in-breeding and where you will not be stuck with females that have been tried (and failed) before. I am thinking here of hens that are plagued with intestinal upsets during breeding, which causes them to foul their nests and young. This behavior was long mistaken for sweating sickness because the hen's stomach is so wet. Even today females that are suffering from these ailments are often placed in this incorrect category. Such females can often pass a perfunctory examination and have good coloring, so they regularly end up with beginning breeders. Buy your birds at an establishment that is not afraid to let you inspect the breeding quarters so that you can see their breeding standards and results for yourself. Buy females that were hatched in that same year. Once in a while we might read that we should start breeding with a young male and a female a bit over

Border Fancy (light green).

one year old. This is one of many old wives' tales that prevail in the canary fancier circuit. A young female from good parentage will do just as well, and at least we will not be taking the chance of buying hens that have already been tried for a season and found to be less than satisfactory. It is also unadvisable to buy at an address where the breeder raised the young by hand because the mother refused. Often a young female from such a nest will be equally unwilling to rear her own young. Unwillingness to feed should be seen as a disease. We should never consider beginning or continuing with such birds. We assume, therefore, that you will always demand A-1 birds; this constitutes an important factor in the foundation of successful breeding.

WHICH CANARIES DO WE CHOOSE?

If we keep within the guidelines that will be set down later, I am convinced you will be able to multiply your canaries . . . like mice! We can estimate an average of ten birds per female. Naturally we should keep the best birds ourselves, those we will want to use in shows and for breeding in the next season. But how do we get rid of the rest? That will depend very much on which type of canary or which color variety we choose. If one is basically interested in fast breeding and getting rid of one's birds quickly, without going into specialized breeding, it should be no problem to sell whatever we have produced to a wholesaler. Every year wholesalers and exporters willingly buy everything they can get their hands on. (The Netherlands alone exports some 250,000 canaries annually.) The prices range from $25.00 to $75.00 and more for a male and $30.00 plus for a female. If you want $75-$100 or more for a female, you will have to adapt your breeding to whatever color is currently fashionable locally and/or abroad. One year this may be red-orange, the next perhaps a variegated red-orange, with specialists asking for good gold and silver

Gloster Fancy Corona (crested).

tones. There is also a lot of selling and trading between fanciers, and the above mentioned prices are for birds who have achieved a rating of at least 88-89 points.

One can also breed with the intention of supplying individual buyers. There are countless families who like to keep a single canary. If we were to place an advertisement in a local paper a week before Christmas, as an example, we may sell as many as ten per day. These would have to be males, however, and preferably the common yellow variety. It is quite remarkable how often an individual buyer may not even give a flock of beautiful Rose Isabel or Rose Agate birds a second glance, yet looks tenderly at a yellow canary with perhaps a black "cap" that we had really set aside. If this bird happens to sing loudly to boot (hard-of-hearing

167

Grandma or Grandpa gets no pleasure from a Harz master singer!), he will probably be taken off your hands for $25, while the well formed and beautiful color bird is virtually snubbed by the customer. He might well say, "I'm looking for a canary, not a sparrow! Canaries are yellow!"

BREEDING THE CITRON CANARY

It is a shame when one thinks of the limited number of lovely citron canaries that are presently being bred. "Why not more?" would be the obvious question. There is a large market for this mutation, because the individual customer is crazy about them. Perhaps the following experience that

Border Fancy; the most admired feature of this canary is its superior feather quality.

Border Fancy. The plumage should be close, firm and fine for a smooth appearance.

I had may be of interest. A few years ago I was breeding red-orange color canaries and Waterslagers (separately of course). Toward March I was was left with a red-orange cock and a (yellow) Waterslager hen, so I decided to pair them up. Apart from some faded orange chicks, I also ended up with two lovely citron birds. In the year that followed, I paired them with Waterslagers again. This resulted in such gorgeous lemon yellow birds that I became the club champion for the color canaries category. The so-called "misfits" with the black "caps" were sold to individual customers. Because Waterslagers are fairly sturdy birds, this characteristic was also passed on to the young . . . an extra little benefit since the breeding of color canaries sometimes produces problems in this area. Hopefully the above may encourage some of our readers to experiment along these lines.

Waterslager hens are generally good breeders and are always clear yellow. If you have a pale red-orange cock with very little buff in his ancestry, you may be in for some pleasant surprises. Such breeding birds are usually not expensive. For $60.00 you can generally buy a red-orange cock, and $75.00 will get you a Waterslager hen. Keep in mind with citron breeding to never pair intensive x intensive, but always citron x flat yellow straw-colored birds. The loveliest citron birds are often hens. If you enter your bird(s) in a show, don't be surprised if the official score report says "has orange reflection on the wings," even if, to

Gloster Fancy Corona (cock).

Border Fancies, 10 weeks old.

your utter amazement, you have never seen it yourself. This happened to me once, and try as I might, I could not see it. I thought the bird was simply a lovely warm citron, yet the judge had seen, perhaps with special lighting, that there was "orange blood" in my entry. The greatest advantage of breeding this color variety is that Waterslagers can be continuously crossed back with them, producing sturdy stock that breed well and have very few dark feathers in their plumage. Of course, there will still be plenty of young with little black caps among them, which should not come as a surprise since the red-orange forefather evolved from the black-hooded red siskin!

To conclude this subject, I would like to clarify one point. Later when you read the chapter on breeding canaries and think back on what was said in this one, you may think that I see only the advantageous side of breeding *en masse*, with constant thought to the selling possibilities.

This is really not the underlying thought. The main thing is to breed top quality birds for the sport of it, for competitions, and for shows. The experience of many, however, is that only 8%-10% of the young will be suitable for competition, and only 2%-3% will be top-notch birds. This means that if we breed 100 birds, only two or three of them will be in the position to claim any championships. Obviously the fancier who breeds in large quantities has the opportunity to be more critical and selective than the fancier who breeds just 25 young, even though many would be very happy to even achieve the 25 figure. Almost without exception, champion birds come from breeders who have countless birds in their flocks.

REQUIREMENTS FOR COLOR CANARIES

Build: 13 cm. in length. Robust and sturdy. Keep in mind the influence of the intensive (or non-frosted) factor. The canary that possesses this factor is understandably smaller than a frosted bird, which has a considerably fuller plumage. It follows that ivory gold, citron gold, gold green, and citron green birds are usually smaller. We should also make a little more allowance with regard to the size of white canaries. Many breeders, however, are already getting quite close to 14 cm. When a bird is larger than 14½ cm., this is often indicative of a cross between a color canary and a posture canary, which I do not recommend. Therefore, the size should be 13-14½ cm.

Head: Can be quite robust, broad, and shaped like a dome. Beak should be short and have a broad base. Eyes are quite large and should be positioned almost as a continuation of the beak. Many birds have a skull that is too flat or a beak that is either too pointy or too blunt. Some have heavy, overhanging eyebrows, poorly positioned eyes, or a head that is too long or too short.

Neck: Must be well filled out and fairly short.

Breast: Should be broad and well filled out, without giv-

Norwich; variegated buff.

ing a plump or heavy impression. The line of the breast must be a smooth continuation from the stomach, without any hollow areas or bumps. We need to look out for a sharp, pointy chest; a heavy, protruding one; a sunken chest; or a fat, dropped stomach.

Back: The back must also be full and broad and form one line with the tail. Rounded or hollow (saddle) backs are out!

Tail: The tail feathers should lay smooth and closed. The tail should not be too long in relation to the rest of the body; of course too short is not good either. The tip should be shaped in a V, but not so much that it becomes forked.

Legs: These must not be too long; they may be somewhat bent, and the thighs can be just visible.

Featuring: General impression should be silky, closed, and smooth. The tail has twelve quills, while the wing has eighteen. If we see loose feathering, this can be an indication that there has been too much breeding with frosted birds. Multiple pairings with non-frosted birds tend to give a dry, hard look to the plumage, with bald spots and sparse feathering in places.

Posture: Haughty, proud, calm, and straight, with the back and tail forming one line. The wings lie flat against the bird's body. Faults to look for are: sinking down, habitually pulling the head backward, repeatedly flapping the tail, wings that cross over each other, nervous and fast flapping of the wings, continuously flying against the bars, etc. We should not conclude from this, however, that canaries that are to be tested cannot make any movement. They may move, but the movements must be controlled and calm so the judge has no difficulty in evaluating the bird's characteristics.

Condition: It should speak for itself that a bird that is being taken to a show is in top physical condition, without any traces of droppings on its feet or plumage or long, uncared-for nails. It takes very little to keep your birds in good shape, particularly when housing and feeding meet the highest standards. It would appear obvious that cleanliness is particularly important with white and yellow canaries. Naturally, our birds must not be ill when taken to a show. Broken nails, damaged plumes, or a chipped beak will only mean a loss of points in the evaluation.

WASHING BIRDS

It is quite possible that during the year several of your birds will need to be washed. Certainly most birds that will be going on display will be subjected to a "beauty treatment!"

Washing birds is a very delicate task. Often on those occasions that I happen to visit a canary fancier while he is making his bird(s) show-ready, I get into a state of complete suspense when I see the manner in which he handles these rather delicate birds. A bird should never be held too tight-

Provide birds with daily opportunity for bathing especially during the breeding season as the moisture from the baths will prevent egg membranes from drying hard.

ly; even the more sturdy Waterslagers cannot withstand this. It is a somewhat different story with the larger birds, such as doves, quail, and pheasants. Still, we should always be careful, because every bird's body has its tender spots.

Let's assume, then, that our birds are being prepared for a show. It speaks for itself that the show cage, which must conform to dimensions specified by the bird fanciers' society of which you are a member, is spotlessly clean and equipped according to specifications laid out by the society.

When the housing requirements have been met, it is time to look at the bird itself. A great many birds are housed in fairly small facilities, particularly color canaries, many of which are regularly taken to a show. Of course even birds in larger aviaries can become grubby. However, if we provide fresh water daily, perhaps with a little disinfectant added, the birds will do a good job of keeping their plumage in shape. Nevertheless, it may happen that their plumage

Two views of a Lizard canary.

Yorkshire; clear yellow.

becomes a little grubby. It is understandable that this may be more obvious with white and yellow birds, with the unfortunate consequences that they would earn fewer points from the judges.

The only remedy is to wash the birds. Use lukewarm water and dissolve a little baby soap in it, which will give us a low-suds liquid. Carefully pick up the bird in the palm of your hand with your thumb and forefinger around the shoulders, the back facing the inside of your fingers. Use a sponge (a real sponge—not one made of plastic) or a soft brush and gently stroke your bird, always in the same direction, toward the tail. Do not forget the underside of the body. Hold the bird so that it actually lies on its back in the palm of your hand; tame canaries will stay in this position without making any movements. This position, however, is not very comfortable for the bird, so it will very likely try to turn itself around now and then, particularly canaries that are not very tame or not yet ready to trust in their keepers.

Make your movements controlled ones, but do not squeeze the canary. Here again we stroke in one direction, toward the tail, using a sponge or brush (a shaving brush would be very useful.)

Once we have given the bird a good wash, we will next need to "rinse" it with lukewarm water, repeating the same procedure. Once this has all been accomplished, gently mop up most of the water by pressing a dry, soft towel against the bird's feathers. Place it in a warm cage, perhaps in your den, and do not put any sand or seed in the cage for the moment. After about half an hour, place a dish with seed in the cage. When the bird is completely dry, we can gradually adjust it to lower temperatures and finally return it to its original abode.

Three days before the show stop giving the bird bath water or baths to allow the bird's natural oils to bring back the normal luster of the feathers. I have obtained beautiful results using distilled water, pure rain water, or boiled and then cooled off tap water.

TOP CONDITION

It may very well happen that top show birds are in possession of a few bad feathers or lose a few important quills a month or two before a show. If the problem lies with the tail feathers, we would be well advised to pull them out, providing that show time is at least two months away. It is entirely possible that new tail feathers will have grown in by that time. Wing feathers also require about two months. Small feathers require about three to four weeks to reach their full growth.

If your bird is too heavy, you should place it on a diet; restrict your bird to a good seed mixture (no oats!) and greens, and start this about one month before the show. If your bird is too thin, then you will need to supply more oats.

Incidentally, before entering shows it would be a good

Border Fancy, cock.

idea to make some inquiries of canary fanciers who have had some experience in this field. Go to shows on a regular basis, talk with the people there, ask about the existence of certain colors, manner of care, etc., because it is mainly by asking that you will become wise! There are beautiful bird magazines on the market today which usually have monthly articles about new developments in the canary field. Only those fanciers that "stay abreast of the times" will be able to fill their cabinets with prizes. This is also why at least a little knowledge of genetics will not end up going to waste. All in all, the canary fancy is one of the loveliest hobbies you could choose, particularly if you take it seriously.

A Norwich canary with "lumps." The lumps are caused by ingrowing feathers. There is no known cure for this condition. Ingrowing feathers are believed to be either hereditary or dietary in origin.

6: DISEASE, ACCIDENTS, AND PARASITES

It is a simple matter to recognize the fact that a canary is ill. If one of your birds gives an overall "round" impression, with puffed up feathers, and has a dull and listless look in its eyes, you can be sure that it is sick. It might also be spilling more seed than it is eating.

If the care and housing of your birds is up to par, you will seldom have this misfortune. Nonetheless, some cases that may occur may require the services of a veterinarian, especially when it involves a contagious disease that is threatening your entire bird population; for a single bird the cost of calling in a veterinarian is likely to be much greater than the value of the sick bird. However, when you are not entirely sure of the treatment required to deal with a certain disease, it is not wise to play doctor yourself; this may well aggravate the situation even further. Birds suffering from serious problems (such as having a single leg, a complicated fracture of the wing that appears to have no chance to heal, a single eye, a broken beak, and the like) are better off put out of their misery in a merciful manner. This is far better than doctoring them up ourselves and prolonging their agony. Toward the end of this chapter we will discuss the killing of birds.

The sick canary should be placed in a small hospital cage in which we place one or two heat lamps and a thermometer. A temperature of 80°-85°F., which we try to achieve gradually, will do a great deal of good for our sick little friend; in fact, it is a very good means of curing a bird.

For the sake of clarity, we will divide disease symptoms into three categories:
1) disturbances of chemical processes
2) individual illnesses or mishaps
3) contagious diseases.

1) DISTURBANCES OF CHEMICAL PROCESSES

DIARRHEA OR INTESTINAL CATARRH

It is the disturbances in the chemical processes group which claim the greatest number of canary lives. A bird in captivity needs an entirely different menu than a bird in the wild, and it is exactly this fact that is so often overlooked. It follows that it is indeed incorrect nutrition which takes the most victims. Strange as it may sound, a bird in the wild has a greater variety of foods at his disposal than a bird in a cage or aviary. Apart from the fact that the captive bird is limited to whatever we place in front of him, we need to recognize the importance of giving attention to the seasonal changes that annually take place inside the bird's body. Research has shown that a certain bird species may consume entirely different types of food during different parts of the year. I will illustrate this with the following example:

Seed-eating birds definitely need food rich in protein during the breeding season (which we can achieve by offering chick rearing and universal foods), because it is necessary for egg-laying and for growing birds. But in the fall their food consists mainly of a large variety of seeds, which have the task of making sure that there are extra substances present in the body to, for example, assist the bird in getting through the fall molt or (in the case of migratory birds) to give extra stimulation to the hormones which activate their migratory instincts. All these yearly changes within the bird's body may motivate it toward gluttony. During these different periods they also consume other food or too much of a certain kind of food, with diarrhea being the unhappy result.

Serious cases of diarrhea are often very difficult to cure. Their exaggerated appetite may at this point also cause them to start picking at spoiled food, which can cause diarrhea all over again. It is best to place our little patient in a small hospital cage placed in a dimly lit location. Don't put it in a completely dark location, however, because no bird can go without food and water for longer than 24 hours. At this point I would like to interject the following fact: from a bird's point of view, the nights during the winter are really much too long and it is best to shorten these by using artificial lighting connected to timers. I have lights on timers during the winter in both inside and outside aviaries, breeding cages, and any other bird-housing facilities. They go on from 5 p.m. to 9 p.m. in the evening and from 6 a.m. to daylight in the morning. Compounding the problem of these short days is the fact that food in the bird's stomach is digested very quickly indeed, while the bird's ability to take in more food in a shorter time is relatively limited. Obviously a water dish or fountain must be present in the hospital cage. It is best not to offer any oil-containing seeds such as rape seed and linseed since these speed up intestinal activity. After three to four days we can mix some fine charcoal in with the seed. After a week or two we can switch the patient back to his normal menu. Include maw seed on a daily basis until the watery bowel movements have become firm once more.

If the above is particularly pertinent to birds which have been bought from someone else, the situation is a little different for birds that are suffering from diarrhea and have belonged to one and the same fancier for a long time. In most cases the diarrhea will not be as serious as with recent-

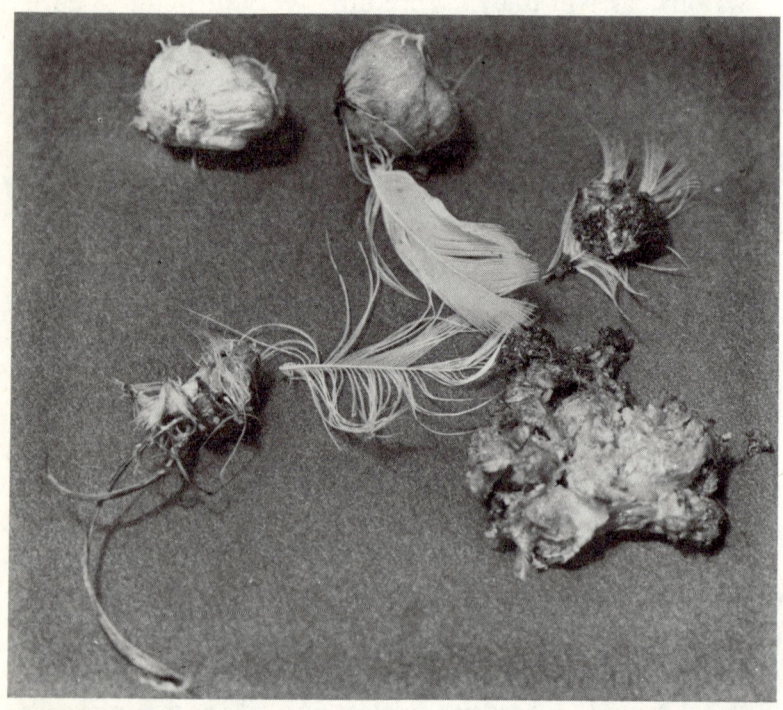

Feather cysts *(hypopteronosis cystica)*, fibro-lipoma (benign tumor; above), and osteosarcoma (lower right corner). Tumors are often caused by infection, but often result from chemical disturbances. The tumors may be clearly visible or form in various organs. The symptoms are serious anemia, a definite though gradual loss of weight, nervous disorders, and swelling of kidneys, liver and spleen.

ly imported or recently captured birds. Often spoiled seed or other spoiled food is the villain. We could treat the problem in the same manner as described above, but it would be even better to isolate the sick bird in a hospital cage and gradually bring the temperature up to 85°F. It is important to try to keep this temperature constant, both day and night. Recently imported birds should also be treated this way, but the first treatment works just as well. Here again we need to pay special attention to their food. In the first place, we must give them good quality unspoiled food and seed that is not too old. We should then mix in a small amount of rusk crumbs and powdered charcoal. Do not give any greens for the first few weeks. The regular drinking water can be replaced with rice water. A teaspoon of sulphamycythine can do wonders, too. Good results can often be obtained by stirring a few drops of kaopectate in with the drinking water. Finally, we can offer stale white bread soaked in water, hard-boiled egg, maw seed, and universal or chick rearing food. A small amount of rusk crumbs sprinkled on the stale bread can give very good results as well.

It is very important that the "hospital" be kept spotlessly clean; under no circumstances must a bird be able to soil itself. Any dirt or mess on the patient's body should be carefully removed with a soft cloth and lukewarm water. Besides causes such as spoiled seed, greens that are too wet, and temperature differences that are too great, too great an amount of cod-liver oil mixed in with the seed can also be the villain that brings on diarrhea. Catching cold can often lead to this illness. Cod-liver oil must always be given in very limited quantitites; two to three drops per kilo of seed are ample. It should also speak for itself that the seed and oil should be very well mixed together.

Once our patient is cured, it cannot be put back with the other birds immediately. First the temperature should be gradually dropped. When the weather is warm and sunny,

Hygiene is paramount during the breeding season to prevent parasites and disease. A bird keeper must be sure to do a thorough cleaning of the nest pans and nesting boxes because these objects in particular are favorite breeding grounds of bacteria. Sterilized nesting materials are readily supplied in pet shops.

the bird can rejoin his cohorts. If we deviate from the prescribed treatment, a relapse is altogether possible.

CONSTIPATION

On the other side of the coin, there is the condition of constipation; fortunately this is rather rare among canaries. The sick bird restlessly flaps its tail up and down without being able to finish its bowel movement. The cause can be too much egg food, bad seed, or particularly, an excess of maw seed. As a stool softener, give the bird a piece of ripe apple. Birds suffering from constipation need not be placed in the hospital cage, but they should be separated from the other birds. A good general rule is that any bird not feeling up to par should be immediately separated from the other birds and should not be returned until it is completely cured. For safety's sake, where there is some room for doubt, we should keep the bird in quarantine a little longer. A bird suffering from constipation should have some cod-liver oil mixed in with the seeds, but now especially make sure not to mix in too much. It should also be given a few leaves of chicory daily. These are all somewhat "old-fashioned" remedies, admittedly, but in practice they fortunately work very well. We can also use Glaubers' salt, available in most good drug stores; just a little dissolved in the drinking water can effect a considerable improvement. Another good old remedy is to add 10 drops of syrup of buckthorn to a drinker of water.

GOUT AND/OR RHEUMATISM

Gout will not occur if the aviary, perches, and sleeping place are as they should be. If the housing is up to par, our canaries will have sufficient flying room, which will keep up the strength of the muscles, while circulation and respiration will be stimulated and activated by a well-balanced diet consumed, digested, and effectively put to work. If we neglect these needs, our birds have a chance of

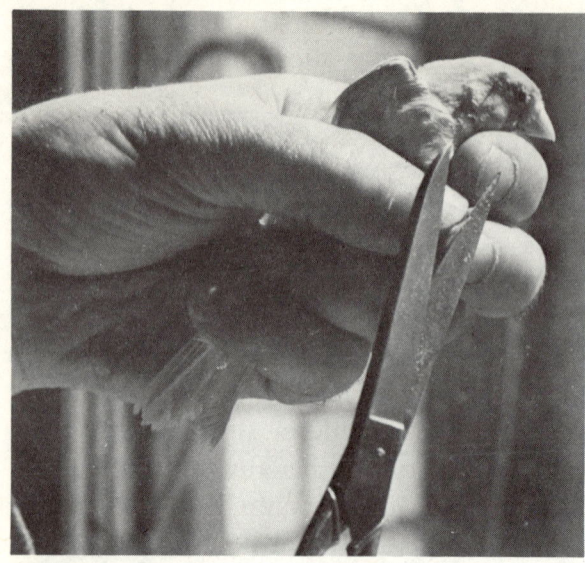

Trimming nails (left) and using an eyedropper (below) to administer medicine.

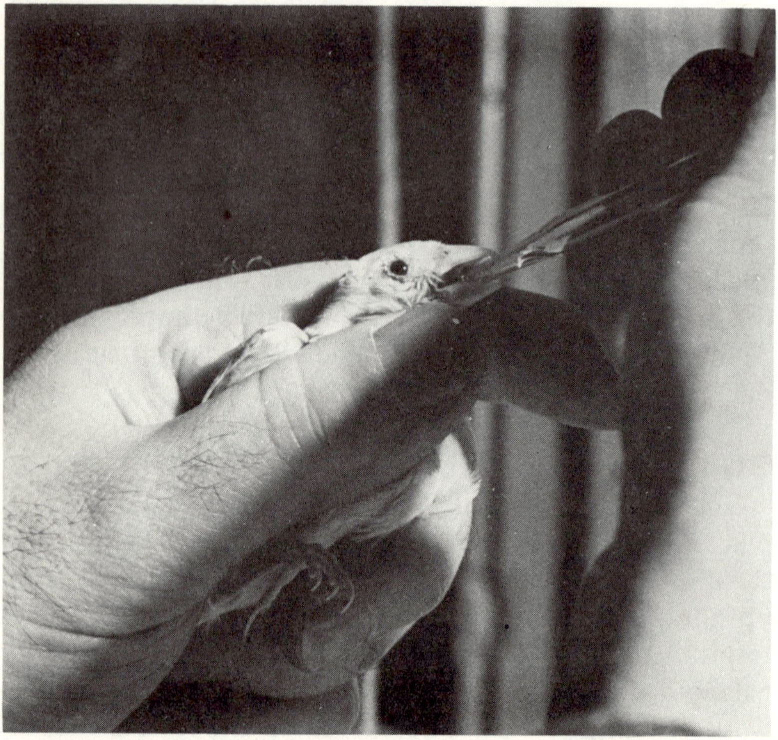

developing gout through the accumulation of urates in such organs as the kidneys, lungs, or abdominal lining (so called visceral gout). Irregular molting, in particular, can cause gout. Movement is of the utmost importance here . . . something to be kept in mind for canaries housed in small cages. Feather plucking and cannibalism can also be a result of inactivity. In addition, the food, a lack of vitamins, and over-population can also be the possible villains. Heat treatment (80°-85°F), pure seed with a little powdered charcoal mixed in, and a few drops of syrup of buckthorn in rice water often work very well. Extra vitamin A, a little charcoal, hard-boiled egg, and rusk are also highly recommended.

COLDS

Inadequate housing, exposure of the birds to draft, and dampness can all lead to colds. It is one of the most common ailments that confronts birds. The symptoms pretty well parallel those of intestinal disturbances. Here, too, the bird will be sitting in the shape of a ball, asleep with its head stuck in its feathers, or on top of or under the feeding dish, rather listlessly pecking at some seed, though hardly eating any, with its wings hanging down and almost touching the ground. The feces will remain normal for the time being. Respiration is difficult, with the poor bird making squeaking sounds. In short, the canary makes anything but a healthy impression. Sometimes he may even sneeze. When birds spend a great deal of time in an outside aviary, their falling victim to a cold will be rather sporadic. It is mostly those birds that live in a damp and often dark and drafty cage that become sick; little wonder! It is our responsibility, therefore, to see that the birds are housed in light and draft-free facilities. They also need a good and varied menu (we cannot emphasize this enough) because the lack of basic nutrition also aids a cold to take hold; after all, with no fuel on the fire there is nothing to keep the motor running. Here also the patient needs to be isolated immediately in the infirmary cage with the temperature brought up to 80°-85°F. If you do not have the equipment to create this environment, place the sick bird in a draft-free and warm location in a vacant indoor cage. A little honey placed in the throat with a small artist's brush can do wonders. Good food and six drops of creosote on a slice of white bread which has been well soaked in boiled milk are the means we can use to bring about the cure. After a week we gradually allow the temperature to drop back to normal. Wait a little longer for some nice weather, and then the bird can once again be returned to his little friends.

Finally, I would like to point out that birds kept in cages should have daily access to bathing water. When they have bathed, however, they can easily catch a cold, so keep an

Materials needed for bathing the canary. Birds kept in cages should have daily access to bathing water, but care must be taken against drafts that may cause colds.

eye out for open doors or windows which could cause a draft. Bathing facilities should be offered only at set times so that your bird will have ample opportunity to dry off before it retreats to its perch at night.

TUMORS

Tumors, often caused by infections but more often the result of chemical disturbances, must not be neglected. The clearly visible growths are sometimes only temporary. Many experts on the subject are not yet agreed whether non-infectious growths are caused by chemical disturbances or if we are dealing here with hereditary characteristics. Symptoms are serious anemia, a definite though gradual loss of weight, nervous disorders, and swelling of kidneys, liver, and spleen. These swellings, as I have had the opportunity to see in a couple of laboratories, can have amazingly large dimensions. Tumors can also form in the ovaries, lungs, intestines, and heart, among other organs. Canaries and parrakeets seem to be particularly susceptible to tumors. Even excessive inbreeding can cause tumors. There is still a lot to be learned about this subject. In the meantime, birds that develop tumors through any of these causes are living on borrowed time.

2) INDIVIDUAL ILLNESSES AND MISHAPS

FRACTURES

Fracture of the spine can occur if a bird crashes into something hard, like glass, wire, or wood in an unfortunate position. A sudden scare may cause this kind of uncontrolled flight. That is why I would like to emphasize again the importance of creating a peaceful environment around your aviary and acting in a controlled and restful manner whenever you are around an aviary or cage. There are no objections to small children being allowed to look at Daddy's birds, and they certainly seem to enjoy this, but do see to it that they behave calmly without too much screaming and arm-waving, which is often such a spontaneous and natural reaction for children. With a little insight I am sure any mother or father can keep their children under control near the aviary. It will no doubt be clear to everyone that a fracture of the spine is virtually always soon followed by the death of the bird. More important to us—inasmuch as we can do something about it—is a fracture of the wing. This is easily recognized, since the bird will be sitting pitifully in a corner of its cage or aviary, practically incapable of flying. The broken wing hangs almost completely or completely down and cannot be raised to its normal position. Sometimes this misfortune can happen when birds are being caught for one reason or another. Catching birds is a very delicate operation and requires some very careful movements on the part of the captor. The edge of the net must be wrapped with foam rubber or cotton in the event that it comes into contact with a bird you are trying to catch.

It will be a simple matter to ascertain the location of the fracture when examining the wing. Using a few drops of an anti-bacterial solution, disinfect the fracture. Many brands have the added advantage of activating the various glands so that the healing process can follow without a hitch. If it appears that only the bone is broken without having injured the muscles and the skin, bring the broken bones together and tape them with plaster. The anti-bacterial solution can always be used even with a normal or spontaneous fracture. After about fifteen days the wing should have healed. It is advisable, however, to place the bird in a cage by itself in a light, warm location. Feed and water dishes should be placed on the floor of the cage so that the little patient can easily get to them. There should not be any perches in the cage ... for obvious reasons. We don't want to tempt the bird to strain its wing prematurely. Rest is a very

Norwich canary. The rotund and stocky figure of the breed which has earned for it the nickname of 'the John Bull of the canary world' is apparent here.

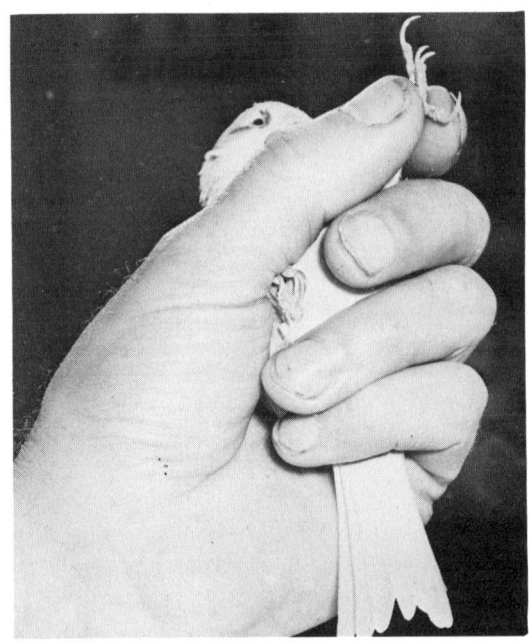

Nail clipping: the claw should be held up against the light to detect blood vessels and thereby prevent cutting into them.

Trimming the bird's claws and varying the thickness of the perches provide a certain amount of relaxation to the muscles of the feet and legs.

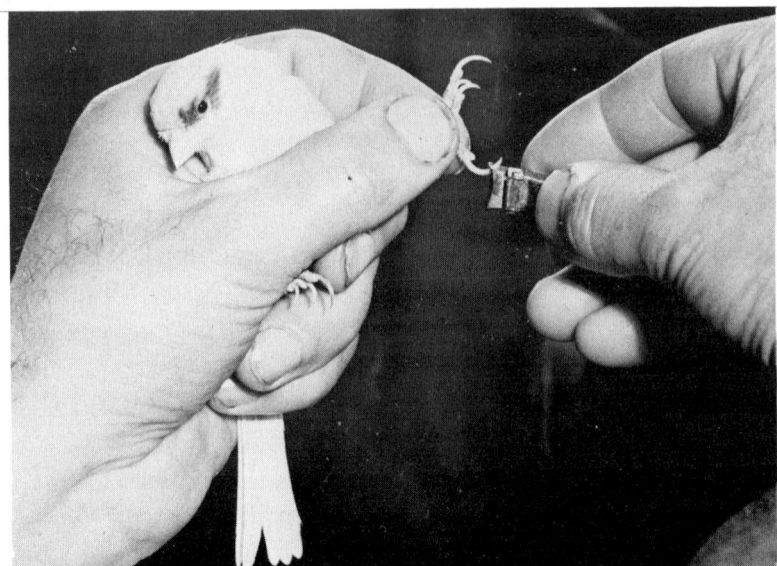

important factor in the healing process. Extra vitamin D, calcium, and cod-liver oil are highly recommended. A little fruit now and then, stale white bread soaked in milk, universal food, and egg food are also very good.

An exposed fracture of the wing (complicated fracture), where the bone sticks through the skin, is extremely difficult to treat. Most cases are even impossible for a veterinarian, so it is wise to put the patient out of his misery, especially because in most cases the end sticking out has the chance to really dry out, die off, and finally fall off. The bird, of course, can no longer fly.

A fracture of the leg is also easy to recognize. The bird is on the floor of his cage or aviary and has great difficulty in moving. Quite often the fracture is the result of an unfortunate mishap while catching the bird or of nails that are too long. We must use the utmost care when catching birds. First disinfect the area of the fracture. Then either wrap a stiff bandage around it or make a splint using a match or a chicken quill that has been cut open and affix that to the leg. The quill (cut open) must be thicker than the fractured leg. Straighten out the leg by carefully pulling a piece of thread tied to the foot. If the bottom part of the leg has been damaged, it is best to use a quill splint about 1 cm. long clasped to the fracture. The splint is fastened with a small amount of plaster or wrapped with cotton or wool yarn. Remember not to tie anything too tightly to avoid cutting off the circulation. A fracture of the thigh is treated in the same manner. The patient should be placed in a cage by itself. The floor of the cage should be soft . . . a thick layer of sand will do nicely. Any perches should be removed, of course, and food and water dishes should be readily accessible. Apart from extra vitamin D, calcium, cuttlebone, egg food, and universal food, we should not forget to add a little cod-liver oil to the seed and offer some greens. If the leg does not turn black after a time, then the "operation" has been a success! Should the leg turn blue and later black,

Gloster Fancy canary. A good type of consort with a broad, well rounded head and full eyebrow.

Lancashire Coppy canary. The Lancashire Coppy is a very old English breed which became extinct during World War II but has recently been re-created by 'breeding back' from stock known to contain Lancashire blood which had been used for improvement in earlier years.

this means that the splint was too tight and the leg "died off." It will then need to be amputated. After a month the splint can be removed, if the treatment was completed correctly.

To avoid "spontaneous fractures," that is, those without any apparent cause, we should regularly give our bird vitamin D, as well as cuttlebone, calcium and greens.

BALANCE PROBLEMS

Both during intensely hot and very cold days, it may happen that some of our canaries have a problem moving and, when they do, have difficulty in maintaining their balance when on their feet, fall, and cannot fly straight. A too rapid blood pressure in the various nervous centers (particularly in their small brain) brings about these symptoms. Sometimes this is followed by the death of the bird, but in most cases these symptoms disappear spontaneously and quite quickly.

We can help matters along by applying a compress drenched in tincture of iodine. In most cases this has a strong curing influence. It is also a good idea to place the bird in a separate, preferably small, cage placed in a somewhat dark location.

HOARSENESS

Hoarseness can have one of three causes: a) a cold; b) too much intensive singing; and c) fatty degeneration (see a later section for details). This hoarseness can be of a chronic nature, in which case it can be hereditary to the offspring. If a cold is the cause, we will need to follow the treatment as prescribed under colds. When the hoarseness has been caused by too much singing, it is best to place the bird in a separate cage, covering this with a cloth and making sure that it is not in the vicinity of any singing birds. Placing the patient with a hen can also very efficiently get rid of the hoarseness. Birds that are suffering from hoarse-

Handfeeding of young canaries is, on occasion, necessary to ensure adequate vitamins and calcium.

ness can be recognized by their difficult, hoarse song; sometimes it is even difficult to clearly hear the sound that they come out with. Their beaks are often wide open. Hoarseness can occur particularly after the molt. In all three cases, honey mixed in with their drinking water is usually helpful, as is grape sugar. A little sour apple sauce every three days can also give good results. Chronic hoarseness is generally incurable.

BALDNESS AND MOLTING

When birds reveal bald spots outside of the molting period, we are dealing with parasites. The birds will do a great deal of scratching, too. These parasites, such as bird lice and mites, must be forcefully dealt with. Bird lice usually hide by day in corners and crevices (often in nesting

Red Factor canary (apricot hen). This is the 'buff' counterpart in Red Factors, sometimes referred to as 'frosted' or 'non-intensive'.

Red Factor canary. A bronze Ino Rose Pastel cock. One of the newest mutations, this bird is, in fact, a 'self' although the melanins show only as faint brown markings.

boxes and under perches) but come onto the canaries at night to suck their blood. Mosquitoes and other damaging insects can cause a great deal of discomfort to our canaries, particularly during the breeding season. Thanks to various sprays, we should be able to effectively rid our birds of any kind of parasite. Under no circumstances should you use DDT or Lindane since these are extremely dangerous to our birds! Besides that, they are currently illegal to use.

Too great a difference in temperature can also cause bald spots on our birds. Quite often we have seen outside aviaries that are partially or even completely enclosed in glass; the temperature can rise so high during the day in such an aviary that it is more like a hot house than a house for birds. The nights, on the other hand, particularly in the spring, are often cold, so the temperature difference is really very great. This can easily cause the birds to develop bald spots, particularly on the back and head. We should try, therefore, to avoid these huge differences in temperature. This can be achieved by keeping the aviary open during the day instead of creating a greenhouse, which would be more suitable for tropical birds rather than canaries.

Baldness, of course, can also be seen during the molting period. Providing the bald spots do not become too large, we need not concern ourselves about them. Molting birds need a great variety of food that is full of vitamins and calcium. Experience has also taught us that it is highly recommended to have your birds housed in a good sized flight allowing them plenty of room for exercise. Exercise during the molt is a very important factor which should not be neglected. A lot of activity favorably influences the growth of the new feathers.

SORE OR INFECTED EYES

You may notice the appearance of this symptom especially during the winter months. It is a result of a vitamin deficiency. Lettuce and seeds rich in oils will take care of the problem. Mix a few drops of cod-liver oil in with the seeds.

SICKLE NAILS

These can be avoided by having good sleeping and sitting perches. Should sickle nails occur, you will have to cut them with a sharp pair of scissors. Do not cut too deeply or you will injure the live part of the nail, which can be seen by the red blood vessels that shine through the horn. The thick topside will need to be fashioned with a new point. As you will see, this is not exactly the easiest job in the world. If a nail should happen to break, treat it in the same way.

CALCIFIED FEET

It is difficult to completely protect old birds from this complaint, although salad oil can do wonders. Young birds are rarely bothered with it, certainly not when feeding and sleeping conditions are up to par. The condition of calcified feet can occur in varying degrees. With a fairly serious case, the bird suffers a great deal from itchy, swollen feet and walking becomes difficult and slow. Mites are the main villains. As mentioned, salad oil can be rubbed onto the feet, but a foot bath of warm water with washing soda added can do wonders also. A little turpentine painted onto the feet with a brush also works very well. After such a treatment, rub petroleum jelly into the feet. Keep in mind that feet sticky with jelly will soon pick up any sand or dirt, so place the bird in a little cage and place some paper on the bottom. Be sure to disinfect perches and sleeping quarters and make sure that bathing water is replaced daily. Incidentally, there is also a special foot ointment available on the market.

INFECTED OIL GLAND

This gland is located at the end of the back. When it is infected, the bird will constantly pick at it. If we supply our

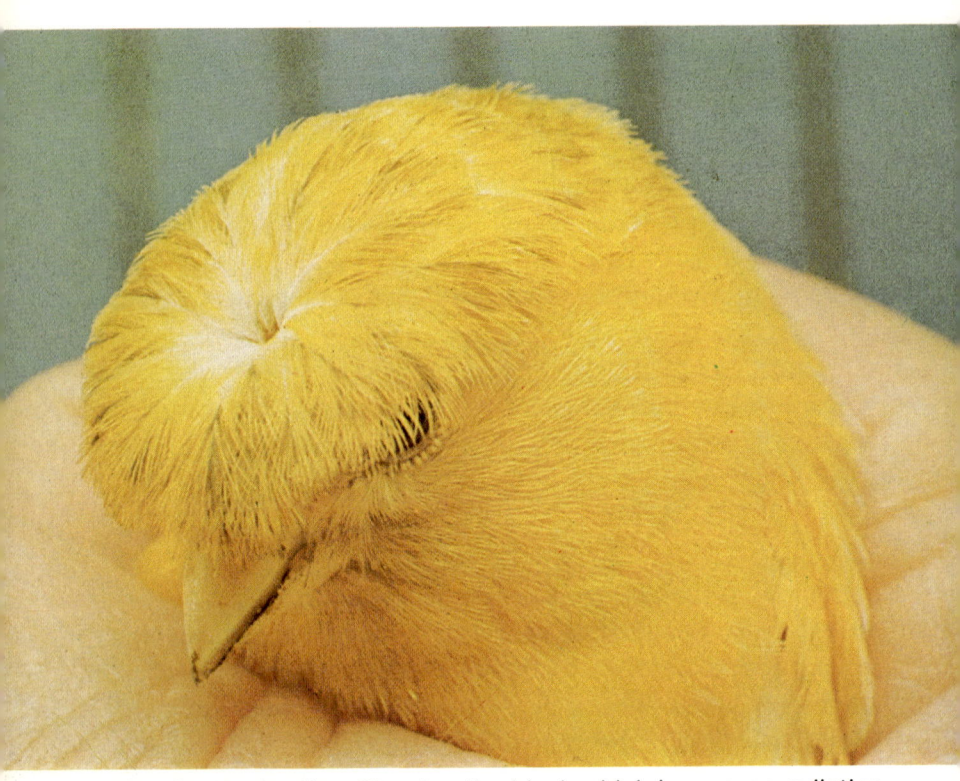

The Crest mutation. Showing the ideal, which is an even radiation of feathers from a very small central point. All crested breeds have this feature in common; it merely varies in the extent of its development.

Opposite:
Yorkshire canary. This blue variegated white bird is a comparatively rare and hard-to-obtain variety.

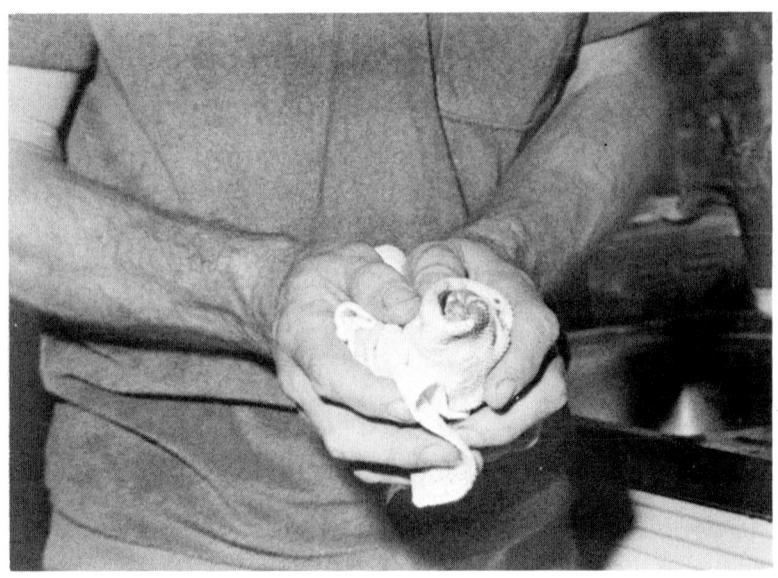

Never force a canary into the bath. If it will not bathe, do not worry; spray non-bathing birds with an atomizer, but do this only early in the morning when the room is warm.

birds with sufficient clean bathing water, this problem is not likely to occur. Massage the infected area with a little salad oil.

EGG BINDING

Providing that the flight area is large enough and your birds are not subjected to drafts, egg binding is a problem you will not often be troubled with. If you discover that a bird is suffering from this complaint, in spite of good care, you can help the laying of the egg along by smearing a little salad oil under the hen's tail. (I assume that you allow breeding only by hens that have reached the proper breeding age.) You can also help matters by dunking the bottom part of the hen's body in alternating cold and warm water baths. Placing the patient in a hospital cage with a temperature of at least 85°F. usually helps, too. If not, carefully hold her above warm (steaming) water, having first placed some salad oil on the cloaca. Don't expect the egg to come out the first time; often it takes several efforts before success is achieved. Once the egg has been laid, the patient should be kept in the infirmary for at least three more days, in a pleasant temperature and with a rich variety of foods. The egg shell should never be broken inside the bird's body. If egg binding repeatedly occurs with the same hen, it is best to no longer use her for breeding.

FATTY DEGENERATION

This can occur when birds eat too much food or too much fatty food, particularly when their housing is rather small as well. The lack of certain vitamins can also be the

Canary which is "dead-in-shell." Moisture from the hen's bath water will prevent the egg membrane from drying out and entrapping the chick.

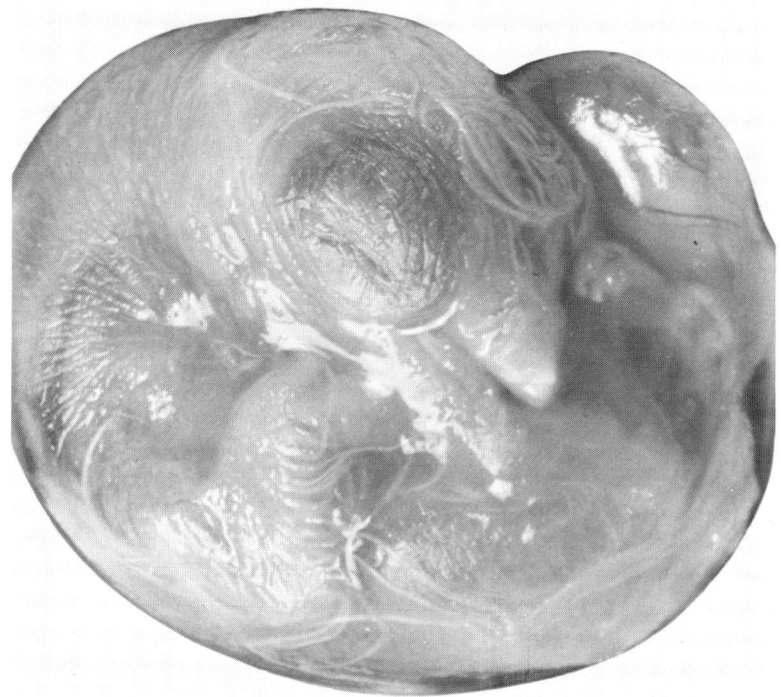

Yorkshire canary. Poor feather quality is in evidence in this cinnamon variegated bird, as can be seen by the 'eyebrow' and looseness at the thighs.

Sooty-Black canary. A recent breakthrough in canary inheritance, this new mutation is characterized by the presence of a great number of black feathers. It is among offspring of a Gloster Fancy canary cock which had earlier produced young with black feathers. It was bred in 1975; the black deepened in color after the first molt. Black birds were known in the London Fancy, but unfortunately this variety has become extinct.

cause. The symptoms are listless and bored behavior and little or no singing. Sometimes such a bird can even develop bald spots. In the first place, the birds should be moved to roomier lodgings! This will allow them all the space they need in which to fly and move about. Of course, their menu will also need to undergo some drastic changes; I am thinking here in particular of chickweed, endive, etc. A lukewarm bath should be put out daily.

CONSTANT OVER-EATING

Constant over-eating can occur when birds are given too much canary seed or food that is too sweet, to name two causes. Often the germ of over-eating is already planted with the rearing of the young birds (giving too much chick rearing food, as an example). Sweet foods and canary seed are deficient in nourishment. We should only give good brands of chick rearing food and the foods I listed in a previous chapter. Dirty aviaries, vitamin deficiencies and the like can also cause over-eating, which can prove to be a very stubborn condition.

The birds act lethargic. They really look rather ill and spend practically all their time on the feeding dish with their wings hanging down. They look thin and undernourished, and their breast bone sticks out. Their feces is greyish black. The under part of their body looks rather unhealthy too, sometimes showing a veritable roadmap of blue and red veins and arteries, in addition to being swollen, hard, and in most cases infected. In the first place, the menu must be adjusted to the needs of the canary and the needs of the season. Sweet food must be avoided as much as possible. No universal food or self-prepared strength foods should be given for about twenty days. However, you can offer stale white bread soaked in milk or water on a daily basis. Add a little disinfectant to the drinking water. All your bird housings must be sprayed with a

A grizzled crested canary.

disinfectant powder in the evening to rid them of any insects and other small pests.

FEATHER PLUCKING

This annoying habit can be the result of a vitamin deficiency, listlessness, boredom, overpopulation, etc. It can occur in canaries as well as other birds such as fowl and ducks. Here again it is very important that their feeding program is carefully inspected and possibly improved. A disinfectant can be added to the drinking water temporarily. Fanciers who do not use city water but well water are advised to add a trusted disinfectant to the water every day. Listlessness and boredom can be alleviated by hanging up a few bunches of spray millet or weed seeds. Other suggestions are: sisal rope, which the birds will enjoy climbing very much, and pieces of raw red meat which will also keep them busy for a while. Beware of overpopulation. As soon as any birds start this nasty habit of feather picking, they

New Color canary; recessive white.

New Color canary; an opal recessive fawn. This is the opal mutation in a fawn canary of the recessive white series.

Healthy breeding Lizards. A calcium deficiency or boredom may turn some canaries into egg peckers and disturb an otherwise smoothly functioning breeding operation.

must be immediately put into a roomy cage by themselves. Once it has become a strong habit, it is difficult to get them to stop. Only when they have completely given it up should they be put back with the other birds. Obviously all feathers should be promptly removed from the aviary or cage, otherwise the birds will start picking at the base of the quill, which contains a vitamin-rich marrow. If this is allowed the birds will never get rid of the habit.

EGG PECKING

A lack of calcium is often the cause of turning some canaries into egg peckers! In an otherwise smoothly functioning breeding operation, canaries that start this habit will, of course, need to be "cured." Boredom can also cause this irritating habit. Apart from cuttlebone and vitamins A and D, also offer them low salt grit and finely milled egg shell. If boredom is the cause, follow the same suggestions made under "Feather Plucking."

PARASITES

Without a doubt the number one enemy of all birds is bird lice, very small biting insects that suck blood from birds, thereby considerably weakening them and making them susceptible to all kinds of diseases including digestive problems. Sometimes these lice even make their way though the skull into the brain of the bird, which of course will bring about immediate death. If there are red little dots under the perches, in the nesting boxes, etc., this is a sure sign that the aviary has been invaded by these pests. Head lice, crab-mites, and feather lice are also troublesome insects which must be forcefully exterminated. If the perches are kept quite smooth, there will be less chance of your birds being pestered by these parasites. During annual spring cleaning, remember to add a little sulphur powder to the green soap suds, thus effectively avoiding all these problems; be sure not to forget the corners, cracks, and crevices! These are the favorite daytime hiding places of these damaging insects, which come out during the evening and night hours to do their destructive work. Should lice and such still be present, then spray with 5% carbolic acid and 3% creoline.

3) CONTAGIOUS DISEASES

CHOLERA

This infectious disease still has no cure. The patient has a high fever, drinks a lot, suffers from diarrhea, and looks very sick and dirty. Fortunately it is very rare, because once a case occurs it definitely means death for many birds. This is why it is advisable to always add a disinfectant to the drinking water. The aviary needs to be thoroughly cleaned

A Border hen with chicks now about a week old.

Opposite, upper photo:
Head of Gloster Fancy. A pale type of crest that is known as a 'grizzled corona' is shown in this close-up.

Opposite, lower photo:
Border Fancies at eight weeks of age.

with a creoline solution, and the ground must be deeply spaded and turned after first having been treated with quicklime. This same method must be followed if *pseudotuberculosis* should be diagnosed. Here also the death rate among the birds is very high. As yet no cures have been discovered.

TUBERCULOSIS

The patient rapidly loses weight, is troubled a great deal with diarrhea and often has inflammation of the joints. Unfortunately no cure has been found for this either. The bodies of the birds will need to be burned. If the veterinarian has diagnosed the infectious disease of paratyphus, the dead birds will also need to be burned, as required by law.

SMALLPOX AND DIPHTHERIA

Symptoms: at the edge of the beak, on the forehead and on the side of the beak pustules will appear. Later these will also develop on the eyelids, legs, and skin. Don't try doing your own "doctoring" here, but get the advice of a veterinarian. It will generally suffice for him to give the patient an intramuscular injection of solution consisting of 40% hexamenthyleentetramine. The healthy birds, however, will also need the injection. When the cases are not too serious, it is sufficient to merely burn off the pustules with alum. A veterinarian can also try to remove the internal yellowish fatty mass; this applies particularly to large parrakeet and parrot species.

CANARY POX

Canary pox is one of the most feared diseases that can hit a canary fancier's bird population. Actually it is a cousin of the well-known pox and diphtheria of chickens. Of the last twenty years, 1961 was the most hard-hit with this disease, and Har Scheepers had this to say about it:

"It will undoubtedly seem a little strange at first that this disease is known under the double name (pox and diphtheria). However, there is a good reason for this. When the infectious matter works in on the skin, little knobs—the so called pox—will develop. On mucous membranes, on the other hand, sores develop which are covered with a so called diphtherial coating. No matter how different they are, both disease symptoms are caused by the same infectious matter, that of pox and diphtheria.

"It is rather amazing that the causes have not yet been definitely established. The opinions regarding the causes are still very much divided. Yet I feel we are very close to the truth if we establish the following as being at least some of the causes: a contaminated bird placed with yet uninfected birds; contaminated food and/or drinking water or bath water; contaminated items in the cage or aviary, such as perches, nesting boxes, wire and bars, and sand on the floor, etc. An even more pertinent question would be whether or not insects play a part in transmitting this disease as well. It has already been established that biting insects such as mosquitoes do transmit it; after all, when a mosquito sucks blood from a contaminated bird and later sucks blood from a non-contaminated bird, the mouthparts that pierced into the bird can readily transmit the disease, which is easy enough to understand. It is also a fact, however, that this disease has a better chance of taking hold when birds are poorly fed, live in inferior housing or housing that is not clean, have a cold, are the product of too much inbreeding, etc. In nine out of ten cases, such a mosquito bite is located between the toes. Sometimes little knobs—the pox—develop on the toes. Contaminated birds soon start to look quite ill, often having their feathers puffed up and gasping for breath; sometimes their feces are almost black. Since the disease is highly

Red Factor canary. A melanin pastel red orange cock. This is a representative of another mutation in which the melanin pigment is diluted and devoid of pencilling.

Red Factor canary. In the 'self' birds, feathering in red, orange and apricot is still to be found and is known as non-frosted and frosted. This example is of a non-frosted melanin pastel apricot.

contagious, we will have to take immediate action and place the patients in separate cages, the cages themselves placed far away from the still healthy birds. The death rate can be very high, so it is far better to prevent than to cure this disease.

"Since the infectious matter is also found in the blood, the mucous membrane of the eyes, mouth and throat will also be affected. Consequently, small pimples (pox) will usually develop around the beak and the previously mentioned diphtherial sores will develop on the mucous membranes themselves. When these sores develop in the throat, a great difficulty in breathing will result, giving rise to the well known gasping symptoms."

It is understandable that such a contagious disease is difficult to cure. Consequently, contaminated birds usually cannot be saved. We can avoid the rapid spreading of the disease, however, by having all the healthy birds injected by a veterinarian. If the disease is somewhat kinder in its degree of intensity, which fortunately is not that exceptional, then taking efficient action may do a lot of good; if our birds survive it, then they will be immune to it in the future. It is a good idea to wash the pox with lukewarm diluted boratic lotion and, if possible, "paint" the inside of the mouth and throat with iodine (perhaps using an artist's brush). Whether this will be totally effective remains to be seen, but we can try it in any event. The best remedy is still, of course, inoculation by a veterinarian. This might run into a tidy sum of money, but we can then at least rest assured that the birds are immune both at the present time and in the future, so we have nothing left to fear! It would seem clear that the birds must be totally uncontaminated in order for the inoculation to have the proper effect. We may have a situation where, for example, there are uncontaminated birds still present with contaminated ones (at least as far as we can tell), in which case we would have to choose the safe way and have all of the birds inoculated.

The sick birds will generally die quite soon—their bodies now containing both the contagion as well as the inoculation—but the healthy birds will at least be saved in this manner. Uncontaminated birds then have a very reasonable chance of not becoming infected.

With canaries, however, this is a little different. According to Mr. Scheepers, "When canaries are inoculated they become completely immune to this disease and, should there be a break out of it at a later date, the inoculated canary will be successfully able to withstand exposure." With other species this cannot be said for a full 100%; this is why I spoke of a "reasonable chance." Mr. Scheepers concludes his article with the following: "It is the breeders responsibility to inoculate his birds as quickly as possible if there have been any occurrences of this disease in the vicinity. In addition, there are other precautions that should be taken. These consist of keeping any new birds in quarantine for a few weeks, completely isolated from the other birds, before allowing the newcomers to join them. It is better to keep them apart a week too long than a few days too short. In addition, and this would seem obvious, do not visit any breeders where this disease is present. It is much too easy to transmit it to your own birds; you could get some of the contagion on your clothes, shoes, hands, etc."

I have already mentioned the danger presented by biting insects. A few small finches kept in the aviary can do much to solve this problem. We can also spray with an insecticide each evening, but this is practically inpossible to keep up and becomes quite expensive, too; in the long run it will cost more than the inoculations. It's probably not too healthy for our birds either, particularly with constant use. If feeding and care are up to par, the disease will not have such a good chance of taking hold, since the birds will have a certain amount of resistance. The old adage that "prevention is better than cure" holds a lot of water, particularly here!

Yorkshire canary. A deeply forked tail and twisted feathers at the throat are just two of the many faults that would offend the eye of the fancier in this blue variegated white Yorkshire.

SWEATING SICKNESS

This remarkable name came into being because of the fact that the lower part of the sick hen's body is wet, sticky, and rather dirty. The young in the nest also look anything but well-cared for. The remarkable thing about all this is that a bird cannot perspire, for the simple reason that it has no sweat glands. The dirty, wet lower part of the body is caused by droppings that are no longer being removed from the nest. Spoiled and wet food can be the cause of this. If the birds are too cold, too damp, or too dirty, this can also bring about sweating sickness. Insufficient greens, drinking and bathing water that is too cold, and the like can be the villains. By providing them with good food, drinking water that is about room temperature with a disinfectant dissolved in it, and bathing water that is also of room temperature and refreshed daily, a lot can be prevented. The infected female should be placed with her young in a separate cage and washed regularly. The nest must be replaced. Contaminated birds should have as little access as possible to laxative foods, so seeds rich in oil are a no-no! With the proper feeding the illness can be cured rapidly.

FAST AND PAINLESS KILLING OF CANARIES

Through the years I have learned about several ways to kill birds in a humane and responsible manner. Still, I believe that the manner described by Mr. P.J. Thijssen in the well known bird magazine *De Vogelgids,* January 15, 1957, issue #13, is the best. I will readily admit that the very idea of killing birds is a rather distressing subject, but circumstances can arise which make it necessary for us to kill one or more birds. Thijssen says the following:

"If a reasonable chance for a cure does not exist, it is best to kill the bird. I had a very sick goldfinch which I wanted to put out of its misery. I still had a flacon of ethylchloride in my instrument cabinet (this is used as an anesthetic). So I tried it with this method. I placed a few

Variegated Buff Norwich canary. A short but broad outline, a thick neck and a round, wide skull are some of the important attributes of this famous breed.

Green Gloster Fancy hen and young. Sweating sickness may be the culprit when the lower part of the sick hen's body is wet, sticky and rather dirty; a new nest is required.

drops of ethylchloride on a cotton wad and pressed it right above the root of the beak, against the forehead of the bird. After a small shock the bird lay limp in my hand. I laid it on a piece of cloth in case it should regain consciousness. The next day the bird was completely cold, so it was dead. We can probably obtain a few c.c. of ethylether for this purpose at the pharmacy. Ethylchloride is not readily obtainable and is also more expensive. Be careful not to expose it anywhere near fire or flame; replace the cap tightly after use. Do not use chloroform and the like, because this is much too dangerous."

Pair of Red Factor canaries and their young; the Red Factor canaries have evolved from the canary and hooded siskin.

7: BREEDING CANARIES

Let's suppose that you are no longer a beginner in the canary fancy . . . that is, you have graduated to the level of an experienced bird keeper who knows what his birds expect of him in the way of housing and feeding and knows what to do if any of his birds should happen to become ill. But now you have applied yourself to heredity and crossbreeding; you were convinced that you could breed yellow offspring using a yellow pair, and the same thing with other color varieties and mutations. You were full of enthusiasm when you started experimenting, until you discovered to your utter amazement that quite a few more colors besides yellow were produced! You found this rather strange because other bird breeders seemed to know exactly what results they could expect from certain pairs of birds. This is why I would like to tell you about the more important things in the field of genetics . . . the science of heredity.

THE MIRACLE OF CHROMOSOMES

Every living organism is derived from a union of an egg cell (from the mother) and a sperm cell (from the father). The resultant cell formed by this union is called a zygote (fertilized egg cell). Once this zygote starts to develop, a certain period of time and a whole series of involved processes later, a young animal comes into existence, or for our purposes a young canary. From our school years we will probably still remember that all plants and animals, including man, are made up of millions of cells. (For simplicity's sake we will forget about the one-celled animals and plants.) All these cells originate from the zygote. To enable such a microscopic cell to "grow" there is "something" that makes this growth possible. The multiplying of the cells is caused by cell division; this, too, should ring familiar in our ears. At a given moment the zygote divides itself into two equal parts; these two parts follow suit after they have first grown into complete cells themselves (one might say they become equal again with the mother cell), and so on and so forth. In the center of the cell there is a partition that splits the cell in half. This partition only comes into existence when the two parts of such a split cell have become completely equal to each other and are virtually two completely independent cells. This partition is not really a partition in the pure sense of the word, at least not with animal cells—we actually find only a construction into the cell wall—a real partition only exists with plant cells. After several cell divisions have taken place, the zygote as a whole becomes larger (morula, blastula, and then gastrula stages). Finally the mature egg (including the white, yolk and zygote)is covered by a calcium shell for protection. If such an egg is kept within a certain temperature range for a set period of time, a bird will come out of it.

Let's go back for a minute to the single-celled zygote formed by the union of the sperm cell and the egg cell. These reproductive cells are called gametes, so both the sperm cell from the male and the egg cell from the female are gametes. These gametes, then, possess all of the hereditary factors that are also present in the male and the female. In the nucleus of the cell there are small bodies, chromosomes, carriers of the genes which determine the hereditary factors. Put differently, the chromosomes are the carriers of heredity. We just finished speaking of cell division (2, 4, 8, 16, 32, 64, 128, etc.), but if this division would continue without being checked, we would end up with a canary which very soon would no longer fit in a cage or an

Border Fancy canary; variegated.

Border Fancy canary.

aviary but would, in fact, need a concert hall to house it! As a matter of fact, after a given period of time, even these quarters would become too tight for it! It is necessary, therefore, that an organism regulate its growth and at a certain point in time cease further growth and become occupied with body maintenance.

The mechanism that does this consists of small parts in the innermost section of the cell which can only be seen under the microscope. This miracle of almost indescribable technique has within it still smaller bodies, which we call the genes, which determine the hereditary characteristics, such as color, of the bird. You may be aware of the fact that every cell possesses a number (always even) of chromosomes, so when the cell is split in half, the chromosomes also split in two, so that each divided cell possesses the same number of divided chromosomes. Once cell division has taken place, the chromosomes will once again regain their original "unsplit" size.

But nature also has its exceptions. We can find this with the first reproductive cells which, as you know, can unite to form a new cell. The reproductive cells have only half of each of the total number of chromosomes, as already mentioned. Still, I would like to make things a little clearer with an example. Suppose that the cells have eight chromosomes (as is the case, for example, with the well-known small plant, hawkweed); the egg cell will have contributed four, as will the sperm cell. When these two cells unite upon fertilization and form a zygote, then it is self explanatory that we now have four chromosomes from the sperm cell and four from the egg cell. If we add these up, then we have eight chromosomes again. This splitting of the total number of chromosomes into two groups with half the original number is called reduction division. When this

Baby Gloster Fancy. No one can deny the ugly visage of this young bird, but as he matures he will become a magnificent specimen.

zygote, which possesses eight chromosomes, divides, the normal cell division will take place, as discussed above. In other words, we will then get 2, 4, 8, 16, 32, 64, 128, 256, 512, etc. cells, which will always regain eight chromosomes. Research has shown that the canary has 18 chromosomes, while the budgerigar has 58 and man has 46. So the canary has 18 chromosomes per cell, or nine pairs.

The zygote receives nine chromosomes from the egg cell and nine chromosomes from the sperm cell. We already know that the chromosomes are the carriers of the hereditary factors (coloring, outer appearance, character, etc.), so we can now see that a young canary will inherit characteristics from both the mother and the father. (Later we will discuss a few exceptions to this under "Sex-linked heredity," where special factors are inherited only by the

Cinnamon Border Fancy; a prize winner on many occasions.

Heavily variegated Norwich cock (right). Cinnamon Border Fancies (below).

The "commercial" canary (above); yellow with black on the head. Pet shops have these standard canaries whose song is bright and cheerful, and usually the bird's song is guaranteed.

On the facing page: Handfeeding of young canaries to ensure that their diet is supplemented with essential strength foods.

Gloster Fancy Corona (crested).

male offspring or only by the female offspring.) Chromosomes possess genes that are the determining factors regarding the inherited characteristics of the young canary. It speaks for itself that the young canary receives half of these from the father and half from the mother, since the young bird also receives half the amount of genes (reduction division) from each parent. The young bird therefore gets the hereditary factors from both parents. This does not imply that a crossing of white x dark brown, as an example, (these are just two random colors that have nothing to do with color canaries) will produce all light brown offspring, since we have yet to direct our attention to the hidden and visible factors, which are called recessive and dominant factors respectively. Both factors are extremely important to the heredity of canaries, since every breeder will agree that a certain color may very well dominate another color. From the example given above (which is not necessarily an established crossing, but only used to illustrate a point), it is entirely possible that there will be white and dark brown offspring as well as light brown in the nest. However, I am sure everyone will agree that the white color will be strongly dominated by the brown. This does not mean that a brown bird has no white in it; in fact, a certain percentage is very likely to possess white genes ... except that the white is not visible ... so the brown birds do very likely have some white, but this cannot be seen with the naked

The broadly built Norwich canary.

Best White, Bristol C.B.S. Show, and Best White, Welsh All Border Show. This is a 2-year-old hen.

eye. After all, the offspring had both white and brown passed down to them from their parents.

Certain circumstances may arise where a certain factor (in our case the color factor) gets the upper hand, pushing another factor to the side in favor of itself. A color originates from the gene. The father or the mother may have a white gene and a dark green gene, as an example, and now the question is which of these two factors, these two colors if you prefer, will dominate . . . which one will be visible on the baby canary. The invisible color is "inside the bird," hidden in the genes, but it is nevertheless present in the baby canary.

RECESSIVE AND DOMINANT FACTORS

When we know some of the terms used in genetics (the science of heredity), such as zygote, genes, and chromosomes, we are ready to broaden our knowledge on this subject. We know that a bird has an exterior coloring, which may or may not be passed on to its offspring. We spoke of an example using a crossing of white x dark brown. I would like to point out again that the offspring are not necessarily going to reveal a combination of both colors. This is due to the fact that the parent birds also possess hidden color genes . . . the invisible factors that are called recessive factors. A visible factor, as already mentioned, is known as the dominant factor.

SEX-LINKED HEREDITY

You will very likely have concluded from the above that the sex of each offspring is determined by the genes. The female canary has two sex-determining chromosomes, namely one X chromosome or male chromosome and one Y chromosome or female chromosome. The male also has two sex-determining chromosomes, but both of his are X chromosomes . . . the male chromosome. The sexual differences between the male and female then lie in the fact that the female has both a male and female chromosome, while the male has two identical male X chromosomes. (Actually I am using this explanation for simplicity's sake, because it would be more accurate to say that the Y chromosome indicates an absence of a male sex chromosome, rather than calling it a female sex chromosome.) In a diagram we can clarify this as follows: (cock) X chromosome x (hen) X chromosome = 2 x X chromosomes = male.

Assuming that you fully understand everything so far, let's make tracks and cover some more ground in this jungle of theory. First we will make the possibly astounding statement that both a heterozygous and a homozygous canary could be identical in appearance. A homozygous green bird (I am speaking here in general terms and not about any canary type in particular) possesses only the color green, while a bird of impure heredity may be green (in lesser or greater degree) externally but in addition possess other (internal) colors. In short, it possesses the tendency to pass on another color (often unknown to us) to its offspring. I said "unknown" because, while the parents of this heterozygous bird were green, they also possess hidden colors since they were not pure-bred. It would follow that when we cross two homozygous birds (that is, homozygous for the same color, as is often done with canaries, except with intensive birds: remember that intensive x intensive produces a lethal factor) we can also expect pure-bred offspring. Agate x Agate (both homozygous of course) produces 100% Agate cocks and Agate hens; this cannot go wrong, since the parent birds cannot transmit a color that they do not possess themselves. The parents are pure bred and therefore will breed true to their own characteristics. The young, in their turn, will also breed 100% true to character.

Two Border Fancies; yellow (left) and self-green (right).

The Border Fancy originally was affectionately known to fanciers as the "wee gem."

In this connection I would like to explain what is meant by mutation, which is a word that you will come across several times in this book. When a sudden change takes place in the color or form of an animal (or plant for that matter) which cannot be explained genetically, the phenomenon is termed a mutation. Through unexplained changes in the hereditary composition of the chromosomes, sudden changes in color and/or form can appear. Sometimes these changes can be purposely brought about, but with amateur breeders it is usually a spontaneous and sudden thing. How lucky we are when that happens!

Mutation should not be confused with modification. The latter represents something quite different. By serving feeds which have certain chemical activities in them or, even more often, are lacking in certain elements (particularly vitamins and minerals), changes or modifications can be brought about, but these changes will disappear again when the feeding is back to normal. For an example, we can look at the intensive red coloring of the red orange canary, which is largely achieved by adding carrot juice or other chemicals to its water or by giving it other preparations that can be bought in ready-to-serve form at your pet store.

Mutations can be, and often are, inheritable. This represents a big difference from modifications, where genetics plays no role at all, since they have been artificially brought about.

In addition, inbreeding will often be necessary in the case of mutations. This means that the mutant will have to be crossed back with the father or mother in an attempt to build up a tribe of these mutations. The parents of a mutant are not, of course, both responsible for the appearance of the mutation, at least in most cases. If the mutant is a hen and the father can be established as being responsible for the mutation, then it will only take one round of inbreeding (father x daughter). If, however, the mother can be determined as being the cause of the mutation, it will take two rounds of inbreeding: first we cross-breed father x daughter, and a son from this union is then inbred with the first hen, i.e. grandmother x grandson. You will see that the second round will produce more mutants. Under these circumstances, inbreeding can be very useful, even necessary; under different circumstances, however, it is not very advisable, at least if we want to prevent our bird population from degenerating into a weakened strain.

GENES

In a zygote 50% of the chromosomes come from each parent. The cock has nine pairs of chromosomes, but the hen also has nine pairs; if the zygote received nine pairs from both his parents, he would have 18 pairs, and of course that would not be possible. This is where reduction-division comes into play, the division of the sex cells (diploid cells or cells with chromosome pairs from which the haploid reproductive cells or gametes originate through

Two Border Fancies; yellow and self-green.

reduction division). This division implies that all of the chromosomes are halved, with the canary baby then possessing nine pairs. The chromosomes hold the genes (in single form) which possess the heredity factors.

LETHAL FACTOR

Certain gene combinations are not or barely viable; in other words, they can be lethal to the sex cells, zygote, embryo (the young life inside the egg), or to the newly hatched chick. I will warn you of the lethal factor wherever this applies in our descriptions of the color and posture canaries.

PAIRING

Toward the breeding season, the cock will be singing his most glorious song, particularly when there are hens in his immediate vicinity. His plumage looks good, is devoid of any frayed edges, and lies smoothly against his body. He is vitality personified, with bright eyes and a full robust chest. The skin on his stomach should be pink, which we can see when we blow the feathers out of the way. It is a good idea to pluck the feathers around the vent opening that are too long, so that the actual pairing will not be hindered. If we pull them out one at a time with a quick short motion, they will come out in a relatively painless manner.

Make sure that the hens you use are always of the best quality. By conducting a strict selection this can easily be achieved. Of course we will need to be objective in the choice of our breeding material. Additionally, the hens, even though their coloring is not as nice as the cocks and they do not sing, must receive optimum care if we want first-class offspring in the following breeding season. Poorly kept hens often result in one disappointment after another. Birds with claws that are too long need attention. Birds suffering from egg binding must be taken care of, and steps should be taken to prevent reoccurrence of this problem. We must make sure that parent birds are provided with a good menu. In short, a great deal of unpleasantness can be avoided merely by giving your birds loving and responsible care and housing. And, as said before, prevention is a lot better than cure. Our hens should be well taken care of throughout the year, not just in the breeding season. During the winter they should be moved to unheated, roomy quarters such as a breeding cage or a small aviary. We will then have no problems when the hens go into the molting season.

Naturally we put together a menu that has been well thought out and fills their needs, particularly in light of the season's special requirements. During the winter, for example, we are well advised to leave out those foods that help stimulate their breeding desires. We should give them a slice of white bread soaked in water every other day to help them get through the molt. If the birds are kept outdoors during the winter, then it is a good idea to add a little extra hemp and coarsely ground wheat to help build up their resistance to the cold. In this same connection, we would remind you that a few drops of cod-liver oil mixed in with the seed is no luxury.

A good hen's stomach is not too fat; if this area is red or purple or abnormally swollen, then something is amiss with her, and under no circumstances should she be used for breeding.

Finally, we should check the claws of our birds, both hens and cocks, shortly before the breeding season starts.

Borders are one of the breeds of canary still shown in natural color.

Claws that are too long on the cock cause him difficulties during the actual mating, while long nails on the hen can cause her to damage the eggs or the young.

Before we place the couples together, it would seem wise to allow the cock to be placed in the breeding cage by himself for a few days to become accustomed to his new home; after all, the male usually comes from smaller quarters. Larger quarters may well scare him initially, and his flight muscles are not as well toned as they might be; in this way he will be able to practice a little so that later he will not become totally dominated by the hen. The female, after all, is always kept in larger quarters and would, no doubt, possess a flying agility which would easily allow her to dominate the cock and simply "peck away" when he makes his overtures, with mating obviously being out of the question. Incidentally, it is quite possible that the two of them may come to blows when they are first placed together, but unless these fights are of a serious nature and last too long, we need not concern ourselves. Eventually the male will end up conquering and the female will submit to him ... gladly! If the two birds simply will not tolerate each other, then we have no choice but to separate the pair and match them up with other partners ... even though this might destroy our whole lovely color combination set-up which we had so carefully worked out on paper! If everything goes smoothly the first egg can be expected in just a little while!

NESTS

Every good pet store will give us a choice of several different kinds of nests, but unfortunately quite a few are not really suitable. Woven basket nests, for example, offer ideal hiding places for all kinds of unpleasant and undesirable

On the facing page: An impressive bird show.

Cinnamon Border Fancy.

parasites. Plastic is much too smooth and slippery, posing a real danger of eggs or fledglings falling out should the hen suddenly leave her nest. I have had the most success with earthenware nestpans (diameter of top edge 10 cm.) which are hung in a special metal hanger. The well known "rope nests" are then pressed inside the nestpan. Underneath this rope nest sprinkle a little insecticide powder that is harmless to birds; now the breeding bird will be warm, safe, and comfortable. Everything will be easy to check as well as keep clean. The rope nest can be burned after every clutch and replaced with a new one. They will also give the hen a good opportunity to play architect, because she will become an ambitious builder, sometimes even constructing a nest with two openings, one for her tail and one for her head! Such ambitious builders should be curbed a little by simply cutting off her building materials supply. You will be wise to keep a close eye on the nest-building hen; we strongly advise against allowing the hen to go overboard with nest building. After a few breeding seasons the canary breeder will get a feeling for how much building material the hens need. Good building materials are fibers, wool, grass, hay, and raffia. Coconut fibers are also used a lot, and some stores even sell pre-packaged building materials and nests. Incidentally, we can also use shallow wooden open nests which measure 15x15 cm. Place the rope nest in the center and arrange some building materials around the edge. The hen will then put everything in place as she sees fit.

A breeding cage.

MANNER OF BREEDING

Canaries will build their nests in and on top of anything; they are equally easy to please when it comes to nesting materials (just to be sure, however, we should only give them dry materials). Unless some strange things happen, we can generally count on soon seeing some eggs. I have seen canaries sitting on eggs in the strangest places, such as in a wooden foot-warmer as used in earlier years and in an old-fashioned wall clock that was not running. A comical sight, I will agree, but hardly the proper place for breeding canaries.

There are fanciers who place a few cocks and hens in an aviary with a number of nesting boxes and leave everything up to nature. Of course some young will be hatched from this effort, but more will be lost because of the many fights that will take place . . . for the favorite nesting boxes, for nesting materials, etc. . . . and through the plucking of feathers from the young or the desertion of the young when Mom and Dad suddenly decide midway through the rearing of one clutch to move to a new nesting box and start on another round! Even the method of using a large cage with one cock and two or three hens often causes needless bickering with all its unhappy consequences. In fact, even having one cock and one hen constantly together in a separate breeding cage may cause some disappointments. To be really safe and have a chance at the largest possible number of offspring, I feel there is only one good method, which I call "alternate breeding"; it is on this method that we will now concentrate our attention.

ALTERNATE BREEDING METHOD

When employing this method, each hen has her own cage and, if we use identical cages, it is perfectly alright to switch them when we are performing our cleaning chores. The hen will not notice the difference, and there is the added advantage that she will be disturbed for the shortest

Yorkshire hen.

period of time possible. Her original cage is moved from its spot and the new clean one is put in its place; the nest with eggs or young is hung in the same position in the new cage and the hen can hop over by herself when we place the two opened doors against each other. All of this takes just a few seconds. Within a minute the hen will be back on her eggs or young. The cage should be roomy (e.g., 38 x 38 x 38 cm.), facilitate the serving of food and water, and easy to handle. Everything can be affixed to the outside of the cage, and the door is situated in the center, which makes things easy when we have the hen hop over from one to the other. The nest is hung up against the peaceful back of the cage. Many people make the mistake of placing the hen and cock together in the breeding cage right off the bat. "This will give them a chance to get used to each other" is their logic, but they forget that a cock is generally ready to breed much sooner than the hen (apart from the fact that he may be a little stiff from his previous confinement to smaller quarters). The result: endless pursuit through the cage, some wild battles, and the usual unpleasant consequences these bring about. No, the best method is to place the hen in a cage by herself with her nest and nesting materials and place next to her cage a cage holding the cock by himself. Next to him place yet another cage with another hen by herself, equipped with nest and nesting materials. Through the bars the birds will have ample opportunity to become acquainted. It is noteworthy that the cock nearly always has a preference for one hen over the other, and he will usually sit and sing at the side of the cage closest to his favorite. In fact, some males are so smitten with the one hen that they want no part of the other hen, even when the time comes for him to be placed in her cage. Usually, however, despite his preference, he divides his services equally.

When does the cock go into the cage with a hen? Not until she is ambitiously building her nest. This is the sign that she is ready to breed and will allow the cock to mate with her. Now there will be no question of any fighting, and the cock does his bit in helping to build the nest by bringing perhaps a single piece or two of nesting material to the nest; in about 24 hours the first egg has been laid. This is our sign to place the cock back into his own cage.

The hen will then have to take care of sitting on the eggs herself. The number of eggs varies from three to six, usually four or five. Keep removing the eggs and replacing them with stone eggs as they are laid, in order to put them all back in simultaneously to ensure that the whole clutch hatches the same day. Toward the evening of the day that the fourth egg is laid, take out the entire nest. As mentioned, I prefer using rope nests placed in an earthenware nesting pan affixed to the back of the cage by a metal

The Scotch Fancy canary, once popular in its native land, is now a rarity.

holder. Carefully lift the braided nest made by the hen out of the rope nest and generously sprinkle insecticide powder. There are various good brands available on the market; every pet store should be able to help you. The hen's nest is sturdily pressed back into the pan and the four eggs are put back into the nest. These will not come into contact with the powder, and the hen herself cannot get to it with her beak; it is under the nest, which would be the place where any lice would likely seek their hiding place. The cock now performs the same task with hen #2, while hen #1 peacefully continues to sit on her eggs. She has to

English type of Frilled canary, cock. Although not a particularly good specimen, this bird shows the disposition of the basic frills.

leave the nest regularly in order to eat. Also, place a small open dish in the cage so that she can also "wash" herself regularly. This is very good to do daily as it helps to keep the eggs moist so they will not dry up. Breeding hens which have the cock with them constantly tend to let the cock feed them on their nest, thus almost never leaving the nest at all. It is not unusual to end up with dried-out eggs under those circumstances. The cock is not placed back with the first hen until her chicks have a good growth of feathers and have become so big that she can no longer sleep on them.

As soon as we notice that she goes on the perch to sleep, the cock is placed back with her. Normally he will immediately help to feed the young, and after a few days he will be doing a better job than the hen. This is our sign to take the cock and the young along with the nest out of the cage and into the center cage. The chicks will be reared by the cock now, and the hen can start on the next round. She is supplied with a fresh rope nest placed in an earthenware pan and with fresh nesting materials; this will also avoid the possibility that she will start plucking her young. If we left the chicks with her, she might ignore the best building materials and choose to take the feathers from her half-grown young instead. It is best to give short pieces of winter grass or soft hay as well as small pieces of pulled apart sisal rope about 5-6 cm. long. The previously mentioned building supplies are also suitable, of course.

If the cock is still rearing the young and hen #2 is ready for him, you can place the cock with her for one hour every evening, using lamplight if necessary. Once the light has been switched off, we can easily take the cock off his perch and place him back with the chicks in his own compartment. When the time comes for him to help the second hen in feeding the young, he will continue to feed the older clutch as well . . . through the bars! When we see the chicks eating independently, then the task of the parents is completed and it is time to place the chicks in a large flight.

As you can see, even when the cock has only two hens in his care, he is already busy enough with the feeding of the young alone. If we use the alternate breeding method but with more than two hens (which I do not advise but nevertheless is still done once in a while), the additional hens will have to raise their own chicks without any help from the cock, which might present us with a few disappointments. Once a hen starts on a new round, it is not unusual for her to leave the half-grown chicks to their own devices, so they will slowly starve. There are very few cocks which will take over at this point in time; they must have fed the chicks in the nest if we want to be sure that they will continue to feed them.

FEEDING CANARIES
DURING THE BREEDING SEASON

There are three areas in which we need not mince any words. Those are: 1) your mixed canary seed must be a good quality product; 2) fresh water (replaced two to three times on warm days) is a must; and 3) the greens must be well washed. It is an old wives' tale that greens should not be wet when served to the birds. By all means rinse them thoroughly to get rid of possible poisonous sprays, shake them out, and let them drip in a colander. When they are wet they will stay fresh longer, too. I particularly like chickweed, which is almost always present in my greens feeder. If you do not live anywhere near a piece of fallow land or near a highway where this weed often grows in profusion, you can always grow it yourself. You can buy chickweed seed, and it will grow almost anywhere, in a corner of a garden or in planters or even just plant boxes on the balcony. As long as it is outside it will flourish. You can also give your birds endive and lettuce.

Next we come to the fourth area: the very important chick rearing food. We can prepare it ourselves by, for example, mashing a hard-boiled egg with three rusks. In the summer this tends to sour quite quickly, so keep that in mind. There is also the possibility of buying prepared chick rearing foods, but some qualities are quite superior to others. To confuse matters further, one bird may have a special preference for one brand, while another bird prefers a different brand. I always keep four brands on hand and alternate them, thus determining the brand each hen prefers. Some will stubbornly only want egg with rusks, mixed with a particular prepared chick rearing food on the market or served just plain. It is best to give a hen her

The Lancashire Coppy exists in the two forms usual for all crested breeds; the terms "Coppy" and "Plainhead" are applied to correspond to "Crest" and "crest-bred."

favorite food, however, rather than trying to force her to eat a kind she does not seem to have a liking for. Where a child is concerned, we can say, "You must eat this; the doctor said that it is good for you." Of course there is no reasoning with a bird, and the result will only be that she limits her food intake to seed. The young in the nest of course get fed seed as well, but experience has shown that they cannot be reared on seed alone.

The eggs take 13 days to hatch and the hen usually starts to sit on them after the third one has been laid. During this time we should disturb the hen as little as possible and supply her with the best of food. Be sure to also offer her chick rearing food so that we can determine early whether or not she likes it; if she does not, we will still have the opportunity to change the menu, which we cannot do once the young have been born and start begging for food 24 hours later.

Mix a little hemp in with the chick rearing food to help keep the hen active in the feeding of her little ones. The same applies later when the cock takes over the task of feeding the chicks. Grated carrot is served often, as are germinated weed seeds, both ripe and unripe, grass seeds, etc. Ant eggs are also suitable; when the cock or hen feeds these to the fledglings, it can only do them good. Peeled groats are absolutely essential during the rearing of the young and should be available in the breeding cage during the entire breeding period.

THE RINGING OF CANARIES

Since it is not possible to enter canaries in an exhibition unless they have been ringed, it is necessary that we know something about this procedure. The best time to ring your canaries is when they are between eight to ten days old. Rings can be ordered through the canary fanciers' association or club with which you are affiliated. Ringing a bird is not as easy as it looks, but once we have done it a few times it should no longer present any problems for us. Take the canary's foot between your fingers in such a manner that the back toe points toward the back and the other toes are stretched together toward the front. Rub a little petroleum jelly or salad oil on the toes. Now place the ring over the toes toward the front, pass over the back toe as well, and continue a little farther up the leg. The ring should now be properly in place around the leg, and the oil or petroleum jelly can be removed with a soft dry cloth. The appropriate ring size for canaries has a diameter of 2.9 mm.

THE CHICKS

After about 18 days the young birds will already have quite a few feathers. They can often be seen sitting on the edge of the nest, taking in everything that is happening around them and allowing themselves to be fed right there, amidst a great deal of peeping. After three to four weeks

The Border Fancy canary sports beautiful, balanced proportions.

they will leave the nest; after another seven days we can consider them to be independent. At first we can still readily distinguish between them and their parents because their tails are still forked and they have some fluffy feathers on their heads, but these soon disappear; with some birds these differences have already disappeared by the time they leave their nest. Once they are independent, we should take them out of the breeding cage and separate the sexes. These can be distinguished not only by the color but also by their song, because the cocks among them already give voice to some warbles at this point. For song canary fanciers we would like to point out that as soon as the cocks can feed themselves they are ready for singing lessons! But no matter what kind of young birds we breed—song, color, or posture canaries—they need to be brought over to roomy quarters so that they can properly develop their muscles and grow into worthy adult birds with which we can have further successes.

Lancashire Coppy; the coppy or "crest" of the original Lancashire was of a horseshoe shape, flowing forward and outward over the beak and eyes with perfect radiation.

8: COLOR CANARIES

Many canary fanciers are likely to read this chapter first. These are the true fanciers who want to achieve more than just a potpourri of colors. They wish to breed show birds of the highest order with responsible colors. They also want to know in minute detail exactly how a given color was established. It is a well-known fact that there is a whole collection of pied colors and, as is often the case with the bird fancy, the more we try to understand the technique of heredity the more we seem to get lost in a labyrinth. You need only look around at a show: there are countless colors and markings and combinations, and it would seem—and indeed is true—that every season new colors are being introduced.

In order to enter the field of color canary breeding reasonably equipped with knowledge and technique, a thorough study of the subject is absolutely necessary along with a considerable dose of experience not to be gained overnight. The descriptions that will follow of the most well-known colors are by no means complete, and we therefore urge you to acquire more books on the subject if you intend to become more deeply involved in the heredity of the color canary (which I would consider essential to become a first-rate color canary breeder). In this chapter I will attempt to touch on the most elementary aspects of color canary breeding and keep things as simple as possible. Yet there will be several terms and expressions in the following pages that, to say the least, are technical. However, if we take even a perfunctory look into a different hobby or trade, we would immediately become aware that these are also "handicapped" with a generous sprinkling of trade jargon with which one is forced to become familiar in order to understand and make oneself understood. It follows that the canary fancy is no exception and employs a number of terms that may sound strange in the ears of an outsider or an as yet inexperienced bird fancier. Without this terminology it would be even more difficult to approach the subject of color breeding. It is only with our own special language that we can achieve satisfying results. Of course, we have tried to keep everything as simple as possible in the hope of not discouraging the newcomers to this field. We feel that the more advanced fancier will find many useful facts in the following pages as well.

YELLOW CANARIES

Through a sudden mutation in which the brown and black pigments fell away, leaving the yellow lipochrome (a fat-soluble substance that colors the feathers), the homozygous yellow canary came into existence. A mating of two light yellow birds consequently delivered light yellow offspring. From this color evolved another mutation . . . the dark yellow . . . which was then coupled with a light yellow bird. The young were light yellow and dark yellow. This was the birth of the intensive yellow bird. The intensive factor is dominant over light yellow and intensifies the yellow lipochrome. The light yellow itself is recessive to the intensive factor. We must remember that intensive x intensive will bring out the lethal factor; in other words, the young from such a mating will die either while still in the egg or shortly after hatching.

Light yellow x dark yellow will produce light yellow if the young inherit the light yellow factor from both parents, dark yellow (intensive) if the young inherit both the intensive factor and the light yellow factor, and dead offspring (lethal factor) because both parents may pass on the intensive factor to some of their offspring. The heredity rules for

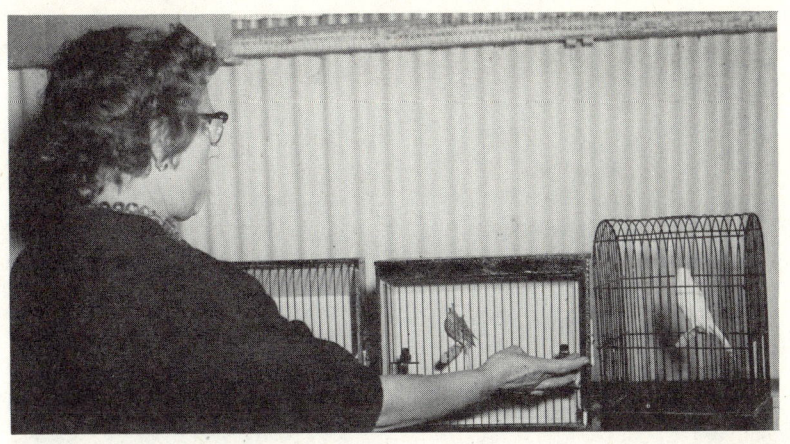
Judging canaries' appearance in show cages.

light yellow and dark yellow are:

Light yellow x light yellow = 100% light yellow.
Light yellow x dark yellow = 50% light yellow and 50% dark yellow.
Dark yellow x dark yellow = no offspring (lethal factor); this match should not be made.

Note: The percentages given above, and those yet to follow, are based on 100 birds. In other words, a mating of light yellow and dark yellow which produces a clutch of four birds is not necessarily going to consist of two light and two dark yellow birds. Nature will not be forced into the corset of theory . . . our percentages are based on large numbers.

CITRON

Among other factors, the citron color is caused by the blue optical factor, which is intensive. There is not actually a blue color present, but rather a reflection of this blue tint. In other words, there is not actually any blue pigment in the feathers, but the hooklets of every feather have a shape that reflects light to give the impression of a blue color which does not really exist. As you know, yellow and blue

Lancashire Coppy displaying horseshoe-shaped crest. At the back of the head the feathers lie flat so as to imperceptibly merge with the neck feathers.

Bullfinch (left) and large Norwich canary (right). The Bullfinch is frequently crossbred with the canary.

combined produce green, so the citron canary is really an ordinary yellow canary, as far as its color is concerned, with a greenish shine that our eyes can see but that isn't really there! We are royally deceived, as you can fathom!

The blue factor's heredity is recessive and intermediate (between dominant and recessive; a crossing between a white and a red snapdragon will produce pink flowers). This intermediate inheritance is proved by the cross between a citron and a light yellow canary, which produces a shade that is between light yellow and citron, where the blue factor is barely visible.

Heredity rules:

Citron x citron = 100% citron.

Citron x non-citron = 100% intermediate citron coloring.

Intermediate citron x intermediate citron = 25% citron, 50% intermediate yellow, and 25% non-citron.

Intermediate citron x citron = 50% citron and 50% intermediate citron.

Intermediate citron x non-citron = 50% intermediate citron and 50% non-citron.

WHITE CANARIES

There are two white canaries, namely the dominant white which originated in Germany and the recessive white from England.

DOMINANT WHITE

These canaries are heterozygous; their inheritance parallels that of ordinary yellow canaries. The white is considered dominant because it pushes yellow into the background, though not completely, as evidenced by the hint of yellow at the curve of the wing and on the outer edges of the primary flight feathers. This slight touch of yellow cannot be bred out of them, but good show birds have as little yellow as possible. It is understandable that the yellow will be emphasized in the products of a crossing of dominant white x dominant white, and also presents a 25% chance for yellow offspring, since both the mother and father are carriers of the yellow factor and pass this on to their young.
Heredity rules:

Dominant white x dominant white = 25% yellow, 50% dominant white, and 25% lethal factor (since intensive x intensive brings out the lethal factor).

Dominant white x yellow (regardless of which shade of yellow) = 50% dominant white and 50% white.

RECESSIVE WHITE

This white variety is recessive by nature, so a mating of, for example, recessive white x dominant yellow will produce yellow young which will possess white in their genes; in other words, they are yellow in outward appearance but include white in their inheritance factors.
Heredity rules:

Recessive white x recessive white = 100% recessive white.

Recessive white x yellow = 100% recessive white heritable (genotypic) offspring that are yellow in appearance (phenotypic).

Recessive white x yellow recessive white heritable = 50% yellow recessive white heritable yellow, 25% yellow, 25% recessive white.

Recessive white x recessive white heritable yellow = 50% recessive white and 50% recessive white heritable yellow.

ALBINOS

The varieties mentioned above still have pigment in their eyes, beak, and feet, but in the albino canary all coloring substances are absent even in these parts of the body. The albino is very rare, since we are speaking of a bird that is not only devoid of all pigmentation (hence the pink eyes . . . the blood vessels are now visible to give the pink "color") but lacks any lipochrome as well. In other words, there is only air between the feathers, giving the bird a white appearance. The beak is a light horn color, almost transparent and the feet and toes are pinkish due to the blood vessels showing through the scales. Do not be misled by the pink eyes, since these are also visible in the brown series (gold brown, silver brown, etc.) though this color is a little different than with the albino canaries, since there is pigmentation present in the latter. I will speak of the ino canaries later. It is sufficient to say at this point that the ino mutation, which first appeared in 1967, is a red-eyed form of canary. The name "rubino" is given to birds possessing the red factor, while birds with a yellow ground color or a white ground color are called "lutino" and "albino" respectively. The albino is also called a "clear" bird.

COLOR CANARY VARIETIES

Mutations and cross-breeding have created a great many

With proper care and handling a canary can be hand tamed.

varieties over the years. We already know that lipochrome birds are those that are lacking in pigmentation. Hence we can compile the following groupings.

Lipochrome birds:
- Light yellow
- Dark yellow
- Citron
- Dominant white
- Recessive white
- Dimorphic
- Ivory
- Pastel
- Red
- Red orange
- Orange
- Apricot

These birds are lipochrome birds because they possess lipochrome, which is an evenly distributed, smooth textured (pigment has a rougher texture) yellow or red coloring substance.

The second group includes the pigmented birds, classified as follows:

Pigment Birds

Green Series	Self green Gold green Citron green Bronze green Orange bronze green Red bronze Blue Steel blue Slate blue
Brown Series	Gold brown Silver brown Red brown Red orange brown Orange brown
Agate Series	Gold agate Silver agate Red agate Red orange agate Orange agate
Isabel Series	Gold isabel Silver isabel Red isabel Red orange isabel Orange isabel

In addition to the above, there are the pigmented dimorphics, opals, pastels, and inos.

I can imagine that there may be some objection to the above grouping. Many feel, and somewhat justifiably, that the agates, isabels, frosteds, pastels, opals and inos should fall in the brown series, since they possess the same pigment but are enriched with still another factor. For purely practical reasons we are sticking to the outline above, and also because most canary show judges prefer it as well.

BROWN CANARIES

As we know, if we were able to wish away the black pigment in the green canary, we would end up with a brown canary. Of course the yellow lipochrome remains. Such a mutation appeared around 1700. A canary that does not have any black melanin but does have the brown and the yellow lipochrome is referred to as feuille morte (dead leaf) after the coloring similarity to the leaves in the fall.

This mutation brought about many consequences; many

Canaries interest people of all ages. They can be cheerful companions for older persons as well as delights for gentle children.

Gloster Fancy; the two types are called the "Corona" for the crested form and "Consort" for the plainhead.

new colors originated from it. A brown canary has red eyes; no doubt you will realize why—the black pigment that would appear in the eyes is missing. The brown pigment, however, is still present, so that the color of the eyes of brown canaries is a few shades darker than that of the albino. Brown is homozygous; so brown x brown produces 100% brown offspring.

The "original" color of feuille morte was a brownish gray, and this has long since disappeared. Through crossings with grayish hens, the brown color became consistently deeper, reaching a chocolate brown. The darkest birds are referred to as being maximal brown.

The brown color has yet another characteristic . . . it is sex-linked in its inheritance, not dominant or recessive!

The Yorkshire, known as "the Gentleman of the Fancy."

ONCE AGAIN: SEX-LINKED INHERITANCE

We already know that the Y chromosome is an "empty" chromosome. The male has a double chromosome (XX), the female has one X chromosome and one Y chromosome (XY). The female, then, determines the sex of the offspring. We also know that the genes (which lie within the chromosomes) pass on other characteristics besides the sex (such as color and temperament) to the offspring. In other words, if there is a connection between the color factor and the sex of certain birds, then we can speak of sex-linked color inheritance. In such cases the outer appearance, the color, will tell us whether the bird is male or female.

In canaries, melanin is one of those sex-linked inherited colors, so brown and black pigments (melanin) are sex-linked inherited colors. If a canary is to become brown in color, then such a bird will need to have a double gene for brown. If brown is only present in one gene, then the canary will only pass brown on to his offspring, while he himself does not need to be brown to realize this. Brown is only present in this bird in the hidden form; in such cases we speak of a brown heritable bird. The hen needs only to possess one such gene for brown to show in her plumage. Of course there are no brown heritable hens (one gene). The same applies to all other types of pigmented hen, they can only pass on the color which they display in their plumage. The pigmented cocks, on the other hand, can not only pass on to their offspring the color of their plumage, but also hidden or recessive color(s). We can conclude from this that pigmented hens are homozygous (breed true to the color of their outer appearance), while the cocks are heterozygous for pigment colors.

In this connection we would point out that pigmented canaries are birds that possess the pigment of the green wild bird in one form or another and at varying strengths (green canaries, agates, brown canaries, isabels, and

Buff Norwich. The thickset Norwich features a deep chest, broad back, compact wings, well-packed short tail, and short neat beak.

pastels). Green is dominant over agate; agate is dominant over pastel. These should be kept in mind when we start breeding with pigmented canaries. An example will no doubt best illustrate the point. A brown cock (homozygous) x isabel hen produces brown females, since brown is dominant over isabel. Such brown hens are homozygous (it is impossible for them to be heterozygous as we just discussed) in contrast to the males, which may be brown but isabel heritable; in other words, they can be heterozygous (not pure). To put it differently: the females can only pass on brown, while the cocks can pass on both brown and isabel.

HEREDITY OF BROWN

Brown, then, is sex-linked in inheritance. This gives us the following heredity rules:

Brown cock x brown hen produces 100% brown offspring.

Brown cock x ordinary hen produces brown heritable cocks and brown hens.

Brown heritable cock x ordinary hen produces brown heritable cocks, ordinary cocks and hens, and brown hens.

Brown heritable cock x brown hen produces 25% brown heritable cocks, 25% brown hens, and 50% ordinary hens.

Ordinary cock x brown hen produces 50% brown heritable cocks and 50% ordinary hens.

One other thing: by "ordinary cocks" and "ordinary hens" we mean those canaries that do not have the brown factor in their plumage and, as in the case of cocks, are not brown heritable. We will need to know definitely whether the cock is brown heritable or not.

From the above rules we can conclude that hens are either brown or not; the canary world does not know of any hens that are brown heritable.

BROWN (FEUILLE MORTE) AND CITRON BROWN (FEUILLE MORTE JONQUILLE)

Every canary breeder will agree that a brown canary with a maximal even coloring has an edge with both the show judges and the true fancier. The tint of both wings must be as close as possible to the tint of the rest of its body, and all this must be on a light yellow background. It is important to try to breed out any kind of stripe effect, particularly on the back; this striping has a strong tendency to appear. Incidentally, quite a few of the birds on display at color canary exhibitions possess the "frosted" factor, to which there is no objection. We will discuss this subject shortly. To get rid of the stripes—common to all pigmented canaries—we will have to be very selective in our breeding program.

The citron brown canary (feuille morte = dead leaf; jonquille = greenish yellow) possesses the blue factor, which we can also see, for example, in the citron yellow canary. Since this color variety is not that attractive, they are rarely bred nowadays. But when we introduce a double citron factor, the results, I feel, are quite lovely. These birds then reveal a deep brown tail and wings, a lighter shade on the stomach, and a chest that has a greenish brown haze. Naturally, stripes on the back or elsewhere are not desirable, nor is any black, which does nothing to enhance the shine. Bill and feet are a lighter brown.

If, on the other hand, we breed with a single brown factor, the birds take on too much green and will not claim high marks at a show. It may interest you to know that the citron brown canary is often used in breeding to improve both the color and the strength of the blue canary.

GOLD BROWN CANARIES

Thanks to the intensive double yellow factor, we can achieve beautiful birds which will draw a great deal of attention from fanciers and judges alike if they show little of the frosted factor (in other words, they are not "intensive").

Chest and stomach are a golden light chocolate brown. If we use a maximal brown bird and a double yellow factor canary, we will be rewarded with the loveliest offspring. The brown (the main color) will contrast beautifully with the secondary color, golden yellow. Obviously we should make sure that we breed those canaries that have a maximum of the main color so this can be passed on to the young. It speaks for itself that if we use good secondary color canaries with less perfect main color canaries, the fledglings will never display the desired coloring.

INTENSIVE AND FROSTED (NON-INTENSIVE)

To explain the term "intensive," it is best to use an example that we can all easily follow. I am thinking here of the common yellow canary. Such a bird has clearly visible variations in its depth of coloring. The breast and rump, as well as the crown, are a deeper and more intense shade than the color of the wings, flanks, and tail. You will understand, no doubt, that a good yellow canary should be equally strong in color over his entire body. We could introduce a double yellow factor to achieve this end, because the young would then receive more of the yellow lipochrome. If we take another closer look at our canary with his not-so-evenly colored plumage, we will immediately see that the deeper color, the most intensely colored parts, are made up of short feathers; in other words, the same amount of the yellow coloring is distributed in both a short feather and a long one. Therefore, a long feather is less intensively colored, since it must make do with the same amount of yellow coloring as a short feather. It follows, then, that we try to breed short-feathered canaries so the color—pigment or lipochrome—can be equally strong throughout its plumage.

Yellow hen and young. The hen attends to the hungry chicks with egg food.

The hen usually keeps the nest clean, but if the hen and chicks look sweaty and bedraggled (sweating sickness), transfer them all to a clean nest.

The inherent danger here, however, is that if we drive this breeding of intensive birds too far, after a given period of time canaries will start to appear that have sparse plumage, and, of course, this is not the idea either. We will, therefore, need to follow the "middle of the road" in order to achieve desirable results. A non-intensive bird, because of his larger feathers, has more room for the same amount of coloring; an intensive canary has the same amount of coloring, but shorter feathers. Consequently, a non-intensive canary has almost no color in the tips of its feathers, and the outer hooklets possess no color at all, giving the bird a whitish top layer appearance which we call "frosted" (frosted factor) . . . a paling of the color because there is not enough color to fill the feather completely. Since it is not a simple matter to get rid of the frosted factor, color canary breeders have made their peace with it, providing the frosting is equal and smooth over the body. Frosted x frosted produces a progressively stronger frosted factor, while intensive x intensive always produces an almost double increase in the intensive factor; both crosses are therefore not advisable.

GREEN CANARIES

The pied green canary possesses the light yellow lipochrome and a black and brown melanin. Often a vague frosting is visible, which need not be taken too seriously. However, a large number of clear stripes on the back is a different matter.

The loveliest birds—even though they will never become very popular simply because of their appearance—can be bred from pairs where the frosting factor is minimal or from a pied green x slate blue or gold green canary (see next paragraph), which will keep the pigment (stripes) on the back to a minimum. Where a heavy stripe marking would be present, we refer to this as maximal pigment. Incidentaly, these stripe markings can also appear in other green canaries.

Heredity rules:

Maximal pigment x maximal pigment = 100% maximal pigment.

Maximal pigment x minimal pigment = 100% maximal pigment, minimal pigment heritable.

Maximal pigment x minimal pigment heritable = 50% maximal pigment and 50% minimal pigment heritable.

Minimal pigment heritable x minimal pigment heritable = 50% minimal pigment heritable, 25% maximal pigment, and 25% minimal pigment.

Minimal pigment x minimal pigment = 100% minimal pigment.

The gold green canary is, of course, also a pigment bird, and it got its appearance from a double dose of the yellow factor and a double blue factor. The most beautiful offspring can be obtained by crossing a gold green normal intensive with a gold green canary which only carries a weak frosting factor.

The following crosses also produce lovely young: gold green x citron green; gold green x gold isabel (also with gold agate); and gold green x silver brown. The pairing of gold green x gold agate is often done to increase the small amount of pigment (back marking), but since such a cross produces less perfect gold isabels and gold agates with a single blue factor, we need to be very selective in our planning if we are to avoid problems at a later date.

The citron green canary has one yellow factor, giving blue more leeway. Pretty young canaries are the product of citron green x brown or steel blue.

THE SILVER BROWN CANARY

A combination of white with pigment produces the silver factor or, to put it differently, a pairing of a dominant or recessive white with black or brown melanin will produce the silver factor. The silver brown canary has recessive white as the ground color, combined with brown; white, then, is the background.

The best cross is normal brown x silver brown (preferably with a single yellow factor and a weak frosting factor), with which, however, we will need to avoid a too intense introduction of green. I do not endorse the popular cross of silver brown x gold brown because of the resultant green shine that the silver brown young inherit.

THE BLUE CANARIES

In actuality, the blue canary is green with dominant white and the blue factor thrown in, which we know is a structural color and needs to come well to the front in the blue canary.

We have already shown that the citron yellow canary got its name from the blue factor that gives a greenish glow to the yellow. With dominant white this is much stronger, so that a combination of green and dominant white produces the slate blue canary; doubling of the blue factor produces steel blue. We should guard against any introduction of the frosting factor, so that the blue effect is not diminished. To produce really lovely blue canaries, we should introduce an intensive factor and avoid any introduction of brown.

Good pairings for lovely slate blue canaries are slate blue x citron green (with only a slight accentuation on the intensive factor and minimal pigment) and citron green and silver isabel or silver agate. For steel blue birds the best pairings are steel blue x gold green and steel blue x citron yellow. In my opinion, the first pairing produces the loveliest offspring.

You need to ensure that the steel blue canary possesses the intensive factor, though not in too strong a strain. Frosting should not, of course, enter into this picture.

AGATE AND ISABEL

Both varieties are mutations caused by the so called paling factor, which lightens the pigment. This factor is sex-linked, which implies that the hens can never be agate or isabel heritable, only the cocks.

Heredity rules:
Agate cock x agate hen = agate hens and cocks.
Isabel cock x isabel hen = isabel cocks and hens.
Agate cock x non-agate hen = agate heritable cocks and agate hens.
Isabel cock x non-isabel hen = isabel heritable cocks and isabel hens.
Agate heritable cock x agate hen = agate cocks, agate hens, agate heritable cocks, and non-agate hens.
Isabel heritable cock x isabel hen = isabel cocks, isabel hens, isabel heritable cocks, and non-isabel hens.
Agate heritable cock x non-agate hen = agate heritable cocks, agate heritable cocks, non-agate cocks, and non-agate hens.
Isabel heritable cock x non-isabel hen = isabel heritable cocks, non-isabel cocks, isabel hens, and non-isabel hens.
Non-agate cock x agate hen = agate heritable cocks and non-agate hens.
Non-isabel cock x isabel hen = isabel heritable cocks and non-isabel hens.

From these rules we can conclude that agate and isabel will be passed on to the offspring; lesser results are achieved with the following combinations:
Agate heritable cock x agate hen.
Isabel heritable cock x isabel hen.
Agate heritable cock x non-agate hen.
Isabel heritable cock x non-isabel hen.
These matings would produce cocks that are heritable and therefore not distinguishable from the "real" agate or isabel

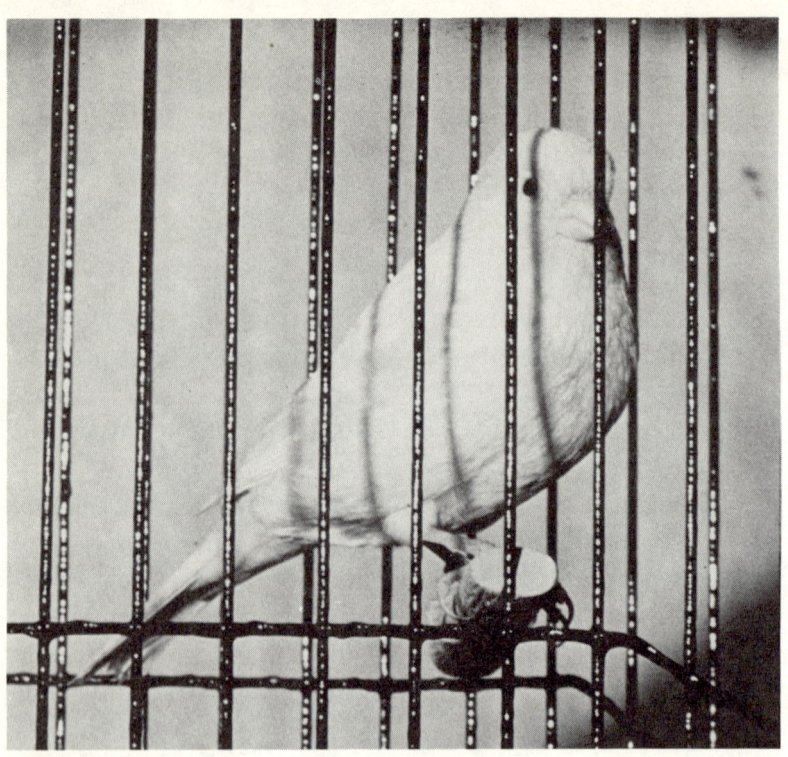

Yellow canary. Mutations and cross-breeding have created a great many color canary varieties over the years.

cocks, which is not desirable for breeding the next generation.

We can introduce the agate and isabel factors to all pigmented birds, but not, of course, to the lipochrome birds.

We classify the agates and isabels into the following groups:

Agates: light yellow agate (= agate), gold agate, citron agate, silver agate, orange agate, orange red agate, red agate intensive, and frosted red agate.

Isabels: light yellow isabel (= isabel), gold isabel, citron isabel, silver isabel, orange isabel, orange red isabel, red isabel intensive, and frosted red isabel.

AGATES THAT LACK THE RED FACTOR

The ground color of the pigmented pied green canaries is yellow, with brown and black melanin added. If we introduce the agate factor into the bird, we will see the appearance of the agate canary (light yellow agate). A good agate has light yellow as the base color covered by an ashy gray glow; apart from an additional frosting factor, there should not be any brown. Beautiful results can be obtained by breeding an agate canary with a weak intensive factor and a light yellow ground color together with an isabel that also has a weak intensive factor and a light yellow ground color. Of course there should be very few stripes. The offspring from such a mating are a lovely light shade, which is logical enough since they receive the "paling" factor from both parents. Because a minimum amount of striping is necessary, we feel it is best to advise against a mating of agate x agate.

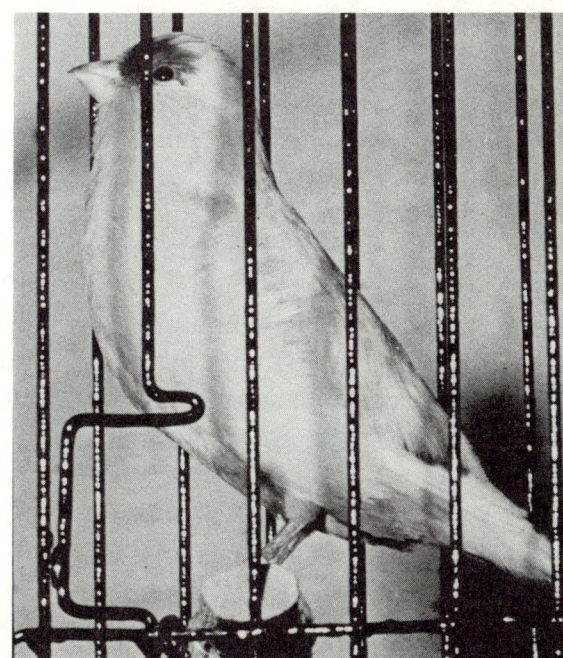

"Commercial" canaries of four or five inches with plumage that is either bright yellow, yellow, yellow and green or (occasionally) all green, have a good song and are readily available in pet shops.

A good gold agate has a double yellow factor and definitely no frosting factor. To keep the feathers short and on color, we can introduce a weak strain of intensive. The best mating is gold agate x gold isabel.

The citron agate should be evenly colored, which we achieve by working with the blue factor. The bird is light gray without even a trace of brown. A moderate intensive factor can be an absolute plus for the canary. The best pairing is the citron agate x citron isabel.

The silver agate is produced by introducing agate and slate or steel blue. The actual color of this variety is brought about by the blue factor, so that there are two possibilities: lead gray (single blue factor or no blue factor) and pearl gray (double blue factor). A brown haze is not permissible in either type.

The loveliest cross is silver agate and silver isabel. The silver isabel needs to have a minimum of pigment, but if we do not have such a bird available to us, we can use a silver agate which possesses the isabel factor and a single yellow factor.

ISABELS THAT LACK THE RED FACTOR

The normal isabel, better described as the light yellow isabel, should have a minimum of stripes which must be thin and not too long. The cinnamon color is superimposed on a light yellow underground. To create lovely birds, we can introduce a weak strain of the frosting factor. The prettiest offspring come from a mating of light agate x isabel. The citron isabel, of course, possesses a blue haze, but since this does not meet with much approval from the show judges, quite a lot of experimentation remains to be done. This variety, incidentally, is often used with isabels in an effort to limit the paleness of the flight feathers of the wings.

A gold isabel will need to be devoid of stripes if it is to become a show bird. A good gold isabel possesses some degree of the intensive factor, which brightens the color as it shortens the feathers. Avoid introducing any frosting factor and, to achieve a good color, breed with a double yellow factor. Gold agate and gold isabel is also a combination that produces lovely young. Both parents, however, need to possess a minimum of a light intensive factor with a bird that has a weak frosting factor, since the end result would be the same.

First days of a songbird—the mother is supplied with special nesting food which she deposits in the mouths of the chicks.

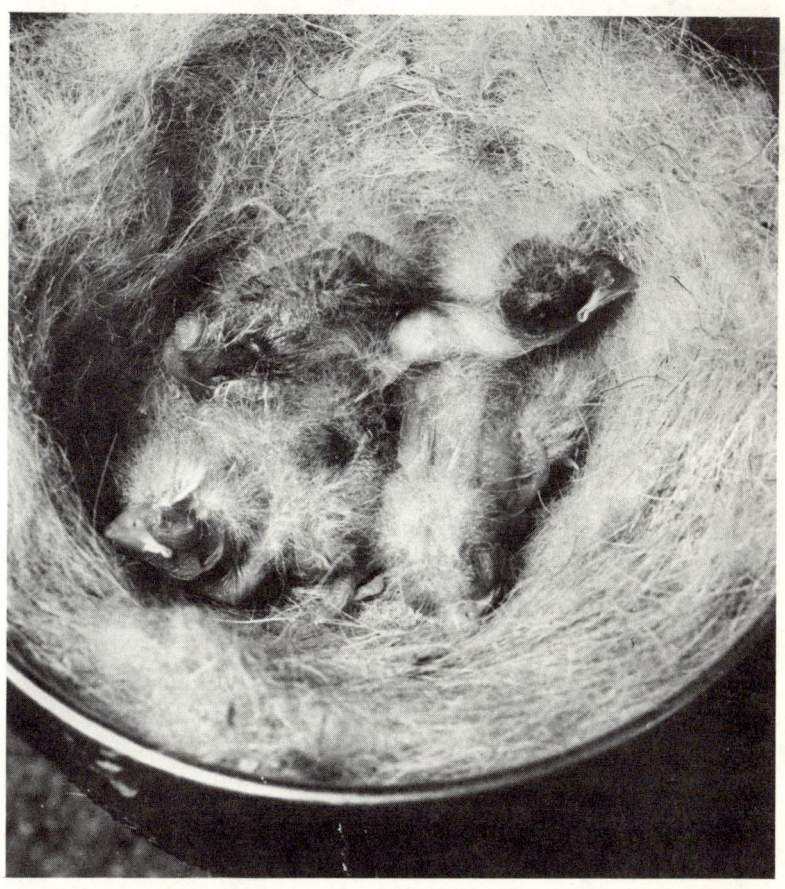

A sampling of crested canaries in a variety of colors and markings.

The silver isabel is characterized by its beautiful, not too heavy stripes on the back, fine light silver gray chest and flanks, and a somewhat darker back. Naturally, to avoid producing greenish birds we do not introduce the blue factor.

The pairing of a silver isabel which has a slight intensive factor and an agate which has a single yellow factor produces gorgeous offspring. We can also mate isabel x isabel with a single yellow factor, which also gives satisfying results, as long as we make sure that one of the parents has a light frosting factor while the other has a moderate intensive factory. This also applies to the first pairing.

New Color canary; recessive white.

THE POPULAR RED FACTOR

Thanks to the red siskin, the red factor was able to be introduced into the canary. The red from the siskin is a lipochrome and has some qualities in common with the yellow lipochrome. We can use the red factor as an undercolor for pigment canaries, while it also determines the coloring of lipochrome canaries.

RED ORANGE BRONZE AND FROSTED RED ORANGE BRONZE (= NON-INTENSIVE)

From the above we can assume we are dealing with bronze green birds with a red orange (intensive) undertone, which combined gives a yellowish bronze color.

A good pairing is bronze green intensive x bronze green, with the understanding that both parents possess a sufficient red orange undertone. The frosted red orange bronze is characterized by the frosting factor, which gives its plumage a somewhat duller effect, if the frosting factor is not present in too strong a strain. Pairing is similar to the previous variety, except that both parents must have a fairly heavy frosting factor.

RED BRONZE AND FROSTED RED BRONZE

The undertone is intensive red and deep in color. A mating of red bronze x frosted red bronze produces the loveliest red bronze offspring.

The second bird, the frosted red bronze canary, possesses a light frosting factor, making it somewhat duller on its back.

ORANGE BROWN AND FROSTED ORANGE BROWN

A combination of brown and intensive orange (the undertone) produces the orange brown canary. The variety is only considered good when there is no frosting factor present, and when the feathers are short.

The mating of intensive orange brown and lightly frosted orange brown creates beautiful young.

The frosted orange brown differs from the former bird through longer plumes and a normal frosting factor. The best pairing is lightly frosted orange brown x lightly frosted orange brown.

RED ORANGE BROWN AND FROSTED RED ORANGE BROWN

With the first bird the undertone is intensive orange brown and the primary color is brown. Stripes must be kept down to a minimum, though they are not to disappear altogether.

With the second bird the frosting factor present is moderate but should be particularly evenly distributed throughout the plumage. The best pairing for the frosted red orange brown is red orange brown with a light frosting factor x the same variety. The first bird is the result of the same cross, but one of the partners would need to possess a light intensive factor.

ORANGE AGATE AND FROSTED ORANGE AGATE

It is desirable to start with a bird that has an orange undertone that is as even as possible. Use a bird that has short feathers, possesses a not too heavy intensive factor, and has absolutely no frosting factor. Incidentally, a small amount of stripes is necessary here too. The second bird has somewhat longer feathers and, of course, some frosting. A cross between an orange agate which has a moderate intensive factor and an orange isabel which has a weak frosting factor produces the best orange agate offspring. For the frosted orange agate we match up partners that both possess a not too exaggerated frosting factor.

A Red Orange New Color canary.

Parisian Frill. Dutch Frill.

Fawn Slate. Fawn piebald-spotted.

RED ORANGE AGATE AND
FROSTED RED ORANGE AGATE

One of the requirements for this variety is that the red orange agate have a ground color that is smooth and even red orange. Striping must only be present in a limited amount, and the same holds true for the intensive factor. Any brown on the back and chest is considered a fault. Special requirements—which also apply to the two prior types described—are the presence of a symmetrical "beard" marking and the agate marking on the flanks. The second type of bird has a weak frosting factor which must be evenly distributed.

A cross between orange agate with a moderate intensive factor and a red orange isabel produces lovely young. The frosted red orange agate should be paired with a red orange isabel that possesses a moderate to light frosting factor.

RED AGATE AND FROSTED RED AGATE

A good red agate has a deep and even red undertone with agate. The top of the wings must not be sparse in coloring, and a brown back is considered a fault. Hence it is desirable to breed a moderately intensive bird which has a symmetrical "beard" marking and the typical agate marking. The second variety also has an even red undertone, along with a weak agate factor and a not too strong frosting factor.

The best red agate can be produced by a red isabel x red agate cross. It is desirable, though not imperative, that one of the partners has a not too accentuated intensive factor, while the other would then need to have a weak frosting factor. To create frosted red agates we use canaries that possess a weak strain of the frosting factor.

ORANGE ISABEL AND
FROSTED ORANGE ISABEL

The undertone of the first variety is orange which, coupled to a weak isabel factor, delivers the orange isabel variety.

Since the bird possesses a fairly weak intensive factor, its feathers are quite short. We should strive to achieve an even distribution of the orange color so that there are no pale plumes in the tail and wings. Another requirement is that the pigment should be clearly visible, though not outstandingly so, and stripes here again are out, as is a brown haze on the back. The loveliest birds can be created if we cross a fairly weak intensive orange isabel with an orange agate which has a small degree of frosting. The frosted orange isabel, of course, possesses a frosting factor in a heavier degree, though it may not allow the isabel marking or the orange undertone to dominate. The most successful young come from the cross between an orange isabel which has a frosting factor to a light degree and an orange agate which possesses the frosting factor in about the same strength.

RED ORANGE ISABEL AND FROSTED RED ORANGE ISABEL

A minimum of pigment and a lovely red orange undertone without too many brighter or weakly colored areas . . . those are the two most important requirements for the red orange isabel. The back should reveal a clear though very fine stripe marking. Obviously the pigment is also responsible for the striping on chest and flanks, but here again these markings must be very fine. The fairly weak intensive factor is responsible for the bird's short feathering. The color brown is taboo, as are pale quills or tops of tail and wing feathers.

The most beautiful offspring of the first variety result from a pairing of red orange isabel with a fairly weak intensive factor to a red orange agate hen which possesses a light frosting factor.

The second type should definitely not possess too strong a frosting factor. The best coupling is a red orange isabel

Silver-brown Phaeo-Ino. In some instances the brown pigmentation covers most of the feathers, leaving only a narrow strip of white down the center, whereas in others the brown is restricted to the edge. Lipochrome coloring is situated between the deposit of the brown and the white.

Gloster Fancy canary. A good type of consort with a broad, well-rounded head and full eyebrow.

with light frosting and a red orange agate also with light frosting, since this cross will produce the prettiest young.

RED ISABEL AND FROSTED RED ISABEL

The first variety should have an evenly distributed full red color with a minimum of agate. This, however, means that whatever is present of the agate factor must be readily visible in the bird. Shades of brown and weak or lightly colored tail and wing feathers are out! By maintaining a light intensive factor, our canaries will have feathers that are not too long. This canary does not, incidentally, possess a blue factor.

The best possibility for breeding red isabels is to cross a fairly light intensive red isabel with a lightly frosted red agate or the other way around. (You know, I trust, that whenever we list a cross, the cock is always mentioned first.) All the crosses of the prior types can be switched around too, but this would seem obvious.

The second type, the frosted red isabel, is the result of red isabel x red agate, with both partners possessing a light frosting factor.

LIPOCHROME AND THE RED FACTOR

This group consists of apricot, intensive orange, red orange intensive and red.

APRICOT

There are two types: red orange with frosting and red lipochrome birds which, of course, also possess a frosting factor to arrive at the apricot color. This color can be found in the tips of the hooklets, which turns them white. If we introduce too much frosting, then the quality of the white color decreases considerably and, furthermore, causes feathering that is too long.

Apricot can best be bred from intensive red (or red orange) x red orange (or red) with a weak frosting factor.

INTENSIVE ORANGE

This bird must not possess any frosting factor and only a weak intensive factor. The feathering is short, which looks very good when the orange color is beautifully and evenly distributed throughout the bird's body. Pied spots on the feet and body are not allowed, nor is the blue factor. This also pertains to the apricot variety. A number of pale quills in the tail and wings is considered a gross error; every show judge will be very strict on this point.

Normal intensive orange mated with a fairly weakly frosted bird produces the loveliest intensive orange offspring.

RED ORANGE INTENSIVE

This bird often displays brown in its plumage, although this is absolutely forbidden for show birds. Here again, pale quills are taboo, although they are generally less bright in color than those of the intensive orange canary and it would be difficult to avoid this. The red orange color must be evenly distributed.

The most successful young are generated from a red orange intensive x red orange with weak frosting factor combination.

RED

The ideal red canary has no yellow undertone but is as red as possible, with the red coloring evenly distributed over the bird's body. Paleness of the tops of the feathers, pied feathering, and other such unattractive deviations are, of course, not allowed. Frosting and the blue factor are also out!

The most beautiful red offspring are achieved from a cross of intensive red with a hen that is red but possesses a weak frosting factor.

DIMORPHIC CANARIES

Along with the red factor, the red siskin also contributed

Left: This Light Green bird's coloring is somewhat distorted, but its streaking is very proper; note the even straight streaks of the underside. **Right:** The pulled-down head and angular towering shoulder are the main characteristics of the Belgian Bult. Smooth plumage and a small, long tail are present, but the posture is poor.

Left: Deep Red Agate Melanin Pastel showing that the peculiar black pigmentation is not influenced by the melanin pastel factor, but only an "over-veiling" occurs. The rich red color seems unnaturally forced. **Right:** Strong, large North Hollander (piebald slate). The bird should be erect on the stand. The frill at the neck reaches somewhat too far up.

Left: This Buff Norwich shows off advantageously. Smooth, rounded plumage must fit harmoniously with the wings and tail in the total picture. The "eyebrow" is also observed in the feathering. Norwich heads are all somewhat flattened. **Right:** This Blue Lizard has bad scaling, and its wing and tail color is not good.

Left: Buff Gloster Fancy Corona with very light flecked corona. The corona itself is somewhat distorted by feathers between beak and eye. **Right:** Golden Lizard having wide and well defined cap, although very irregular scales.

the dimorphic factor to canaries, which also becomes visible when combined with the frosting factor. The dimorphic factor is also the cause of the introduction of sexual dimorphism in canaries. (Sexual dimorphism is the difference in appearance between cock and hen, for example, a male and female orange weaver during the breeding season, when the hen looks much like a sparrow, while the cock is a beautiful black with orange.) The dimorphic factor, then, is sex-linked. The characteristics of this factor first become visible after the initial molt. For dimorphic lipochrome (blank dimorphic) it is best to stick with the following combinations:
(cock) Dimorphic (or dimorphic heritable) x (hen) dimorphic
(cock) Dimorphic x (hen) apricot
(cock) Dimorphic x (hen) frosted red orange
(cock) Dimorphic x (hen) frosted red

In the last combination we will see the sex-linked heredity appear, so it is wise to use a dimorphic cock (as we have noted) rather than dimorphic hen.

PIGMENTED DIMORPHIC

The dimorphic factor can be introduced into all pigmented birds. It is advisable to stay with the following mating: dimorphic (or pigmented dimorphic) x pigmented dimorphic. To arrive at pigmented dimorphic we cross pigmented dimorphic x lipochrome dimorphic. There are a few gorgeous color varieties, namely: dimorphic bronze, dimorphic agate, dimorphic isabel, and dimorphic brown.

THE PASTEL FACTOR

The pastel factor is a "paling" factor (particularly for black melanin), or to put it more scientifically, a reduction factor. Pastel, then, can be introduced to green, brown, agate and isabel canaries, or to put it another way, to the pigmented birds if they possess red or yellow lipochrome.

Stork has this to say about the pastel factor:

"A green canary with a first 'paling' factor or reduction factor is an agate canary. When the green canary receives a second paling factor or pastel factor, then we can speak of green pastel. The difference between these two birds is that the Agate (green Agate) through the paling or reduction of the brown melanin arrives at a color that reminds one of burnt peat. One also understands that the requirement of the agate is that there must not be much brown visible in the wings, because this would indicate that the Agate factor has not done its job very well, and that, in fact, there is something amiss with the Agate factor of the canary.

"The green pastel, on the other hand, possesses a second reduction factor which particularly affects the black melanin. This reduction factor reduces the number of melanin grains and spreads them out; the result of this is that the striping, which is mainly caused by the black melanin in pigment canaries without a reduction factor, is much more limited in the pastel canary. The green pastel canary, then, reveals much less striping, and the black which in a green canary contributes in part to a good color is much lighter . . . more like gray.

"It speaks for itself that the color of the green canary is going to suffer somewhat with a second reduction factor, and has a tendency to become brownish.

"With the Agate pastel we are dealing with a first plus a second reduction factor. The first reduction factor brought about the Agate effect, while the second factor brought about the Agate pastel.

"With the brown pastel, the pastel factor 'attacked' the brown melanin with the consequence that the brown pastel canary is considerably less brown, while the striping has disappeared for the most part. The Isabel pastel also possesses both reduction factors, with the brown melanin having been attacked twice, as it were, with a

Left: Light Red and Black; color and position of the wing and tail correct. The conspicuous light flank is a defect. **Right:** Deep Bronze, a color that represents a developmental step towards the basic Red Factor. This bird has beautiful coloration but a bad head.

Left: Light Yellow Brown having the pigmentation is equally evident in the small feathers. It is to be noted that the dark coloration does not come out too deep brown in basically yellow brown birds. **Right:** Deep Golden Isabel Melanin Pastel; the melanin pigmentation is visible only at the wings and tail.

Left; Deep Bronze Agate Opal; the typical intensive bird should show its rich coloration evenly. **Right:** Light Red Brown Melanin Pastel having fine color characteristics, beautiful in all parts.

Left: Light Red Lipochrome Pastel Opal; all the color markings are visible but weakened by the special factors. **Right:** Light Red Agate; this bird has fairly even rich coloration and very beautiful, short streaking. The "Mottling" is somewhat uneven and its shape is marred by the protruding breast.

stripeless, very light bird being the result.

"With the pastel canary we are dealing with an unchanged ground color of lipochrome. Because the final color of the bird is the result of the impression the combination of both the pigment and lipochrome makes on our vision, we see pastel. We could compare it to a box of water colors: if we mix brown with white, we end up with beige, and if we add a little red, we will get a reddish beige.

"With the green pastels, the reduced pigment color is grayish; with the Agate pastels it is blue-gray; the brown pastels end up beige, and the Isabel pastels a very light beige."

THE IVORY FACTOR

This mutation, which originated around 1950, causes a change in the structure of the feathers. The layer of keratin in the hooklets becomes thicker and the little hooks (which indeed affix themselves like little hooks to the barbules) are devoid of any color. We all know that the actual lipochrome of an ordinary canary is located not only in the barbules but also in the hooklets of the feathers. The ivory canary has the lipochrome only in the barbules, which reduces the strength of the color. But this is not the only reason; the thick layer of keratin also reduces the visibility of the color. The ivory factor, in other words, has a double effect: it weakens the color and produces a thicker layer of keratin.

You will understand, of course, that a light yellow canary, as an example, which has the ivory factor, is quite a bit lighter than a dark yellow canary with this factor.

The ivory factor can be introduced to lipochrome and pigment canaries alike, though in the latter group the pigment plays no role in the determination of the color of the ivory. The ivory factor is sex-linked; in other words, there are no ivory heritable hens . . . hens only possess the ivory factor in their outer appearance.

THE OPAL FACTOR

In 1949 a mutation took place in Germany called the "opal mutation." Here again this mutation changed the configuration of the barbules of the feathers. The opal canary feather is darker on the underside than on the top side because it has black melanin in the core of the barbule while on the underside of the cortex (outer layer of keratin) there are pigment grains. Unfortunately this mutation has not become very popular as yet, so there is little sense in delving more deeply into this factor.

THE INOS

Ino male x ino female = 100% ino.

Ino male x normal female, or normal male x ino female = all normal but carrying the ino factor (normal/ino).

Normal male/ino x ino female, or ino male x normal female/ino = 50% ino and 50% normal/ino.

Normal male/ino x normal female/ino = 25% normal, 50% normal/ino and 25% ino.

Normal male/ino x normal female, or normal male x normal female/ino = all normal young, 50% of which will carry the ino factor.

POSSIBLE CROSSES WITH WILD SONGBIRDS

In conclusion of this chapter, we would like to list a number of wild songbirds that may be crossbred with the canary. This branch of the canary fancy certainly has many interesting aspects.

Linnet x canary
Siskin x canary
Green finch x canary
Canary x green finch

Red sparrow x canary
Finch x canary
Yellowhammer x canary
Goldfinch x canary
Redpoll x canary

Left: Deep Golden Brown; this typical dark bird shows a weak form, thin wispy plumage and a small head. **Right:** Light Red and Black Lipochrome Pastel. The color of the photo is not entirely correct, but the dark color and the streaking on the back nevertheless are very beautiful.

Left: Light Green Agate Melanin Pastel, typical in form and plumage. The head is beautiful. **Right:** Red Agate Lipochrome Melanin Pastel; due to the combination of different special factors this color is very difficult to recognize.

Left: Red Lizard, a difficult piebald breed in which keeping the diluted red factor is the aim. **Right:** Deep Red and Black Lipochrome Pastel, beautifully shown in the picture. The light of the flash unfortunately has lightened the beak very much.

Left: Paris Frill, moderately curled. This bird's head, neck and tail are defective. **Right:** Silver Isabel Opal; this combination of dark pigments makes the bird appear very pale. The white background sets off the fine grayish marking of the top side.

Cape canary x canary (especially with gold agate)
Mozambique siskin x canary (especially dominant white)
Alario finch x canary (especially dominant white)
Black-hooded red siskin x canary (obviously!!)
Black-headed siskin x canary
Mexican red sparrow x canary (Yorkshire)
Greenfinch x canary (Norwich)
European canary x canary (Gloster corona)

9: FORM AND POSTURE CANARIES

Under the influence of feeding, housing, cross-breeding, and selection, the wild canary has undergone all kinds of mutations. Dutch, Belgian, and French canary breeders have used every change that took place over the last century, particularly when it concerned the structure or shape of the bird's plumage, and also when a bird showed a change in body build. It would follow that eventually local breeds evolved. The English breeders, who originally applied themselves to the color varieties, became interested in the changes in shape that were taking place. We are thinking in this instance of the sturdy Norwich canary, known for its size, the "small" Gloster canary, the large Lancashire canary that is bred both with and without a crest, and the Scotch Fancy, which with its half-moon shape and high shoulders will always draw a lot of attention.

The frilled canaries are a special breed all their own, too, with their tightly curled feathers and long legs. When one is really interested in the form and posture canaries, a most wonderful show to be able to experience is the grandiose Parisian show "La Nationale" (Societe Serinophile et Ornithologique), held in December, which enjoys international acclaim. Interest in form and posture canaries is on the rise again after a plunging decline after World War II. This show is well worth visiting, not only because much can be learned from viewing the often bizarre shapes, but even more so because it gives us an idea just how much has been achieved by serious-minded fanciers with the wild canary in a relatively short period of time.

Left: Deep Red Agate Lipochrome Pastel; the photo shows a typical agate bird's head markings. The eye streak and "beard" are very beautiful. **Right:** Paris Frill; the curls stand out more in pale-colored birds. The farther the individual curly part projects, the better the quality.

Left: Deep Golden yellow showing very good quality of form, well shaped blackline, distinct neck and harmoniously fitting head characters. **Right:** Red Isabel showing beautiful characters in the color and plumage. Posture of the bird not ideal with regard to the upper side.

Left: Red Mosaic hen. This outstanding hen coloration is not simple to obtain in breeding. **Right:** Gloster Fancy Consort having completely outstanding form and posture. Charming white-slate piebald (cap-swallowtail), which is also desired in the corona.

Left: Silver Brown Phaeo-Ino; in spite of the red eye color the bird has dark pigments which are exclusively Phaeomelanine. **Right:** Silver Agate: with the thinning out of the density of the melanin the white background of the agate bird appears very charming.

THE BELGIAN BULT

This is one of the oldest canaries. Its origin is not entirely clear, but it is presumed that it evolved from the Mechelse Waterslager. The arched back can still be found in this song canary. Through mutation, selection, and adjustment, the Waterslager eventually evolved into the Belgische (Belgian) Bult.

The "place of birth" of this posture canary was most likely Ghent and surroundings, next to Brugge and Antwerp. The Belgische Bult is supposed to have been perfected by the turn of the 16th to 17th century. In 1700 it was called "Grote Vogel" (large bird) and also "Gentse vogel" (bird from Ghent). The English became particularly interested in this bird and soon called him the "Belgian bird." Thousands of birds were sold to the British, who unfortunately did not pursue perfection in this bird but, instead, used it to breed new posture canaries so intensively that there soon was insufficient breeding material left in Belgium.

High points in the breeding history of the Bult were the years 1700, 1840, and 1890. Older fanciers still speak with passion and conviction of the beautiful white birds that were shown at the Belgian exhibitions between 1890 and 1900. Alas, both World Wars caused many of the Belgian Bult variety to disappear; breeding was also at a standstill, of course. As an example, I heard from an experienced posture canary breeder that he never saw any Belgian Bults in either the Netherlands or Belgium during the Second World War, but just a few specimens in Spain. Between the two World Wars breeding did not take place on any great scale. A few fanciers did take care, though, that the race did not become totally extinct, and at the moment there are a number of fanciers in the Netherlands and Belgium who breed this amazing variety, thanks to Mr. Dawans, who greatly promoted their popularity.

Characteristics:
- head: small, sleek in shape, giving a ' snaky ' appearance.
- neck: long, thin, and elongated.
- shoulders: high, but not giving a bony appearance; in other words, well filled.
- back: long, broad and vertical.
- body: long, narrow with high shoulders.
- breast: well filled and thrust forward.
- wings: long and closed; the wings should touch each other without crossing over.
- tail: straight down, long, and closed.
- legs: long, stretched out, and with well feathered thighs.
- plumage: smooth and without frills; closed; the breast feathers may stick out just a little due to the build of the bird, and this cannot be avoided.
- length: 17-18 cm. from the tip of the tail to the tip of the beak.
- position: the best bird is the one which looks like a figure seven when it is placed in the training cage. It should stand high on its legs, with the neck slightly lowered. The tail should just barely touch the perch.

Scale of Points (Confederation Ornithologique Mondiale (COM))

1. Position:

Position (10 points): Comfortable and confident.
Neck (10 points): Fine and well elongated.
Legs (4 points): Upright and stiff.
Shoulders (10 points): High.
Head (6 points): Lowered.

2. Form:

Head (3 points): Small, oval, narrow and sleek.
Neck (10 points): Long, refined, and extended.
Shoulders (10 points): High, well set, and well filled.
Back (5 points): Long, broad, well filled, and upright.
Body (5 points): Long and tapering.

Left: Gloster Fancy Corona; the bird's form, plumage and general type are good. **Right:** Silver Agate showing poor posture but good large feathering.

Left: Yorkshire; this bird's posture should be even straighter, more **rigidly elevated** at the joint. **Right:** Light Red; the rough, luxuriant **and "frosty"** plumage is peculiar to this bird.

Left: Light Red Isabel, a delicate shade which up to now has been rarely bred. **Right:** Deep Red Isabel showing outstanding plumage quality.

Left: Gibber Italicus; naked skin areas at the legs and breast are visible through the sparse thin plumage. **Right:** Red Isabel Mosaic hen; the plumage under the side is somewhat shaggy and loose. Other defects appear as well.

Breast (5 points): Prominent and well filled.
Wings (5 points): Long, tightly folded, touching without crossing.
Tail (3 points): Long, upright, closely folded, stiff, and closed at the tip.
Legs (4 points): Long, slim, and upright.
Plumage (6 points): Smooth, without frills.
Size (4 points): 17 to 18 cm. from the tip of the beak to the end of the tail.
Total—100 points.

THE YORKSHIRE

This "gentleman of the fancy" can be considered the favorite of the English canary fancy, and when we examine this proud and impressive bird, we can see why. This posture canary is said to have first appeared on the scene in Yorkshire around 1870, especially in Bradford, although the intention was not to create a new breed but rather to improve upon the Lancashire. Three important breeds have helped to bring about the Yorkshire Canary; these are the Lancashire, the Belgian Bult (also called Bossu Belge), and the Norwich. It would appear that everything did not go as smoothly as it might have with the developing of the Yorkshire, and it was not until a decade before the Second World War that the desired results were achieved. If it was desirable before the turn of the century that this bird should "be able to pass through the wedding band of a canary fancier," they are currently a great deal larger.

Characteristics:
-head and neck: full, round head; the skull must definitely not be flat, preferably somewhat on the broad side. Short, thick, well filled neck.
-body: well rounded and gradually tapering; "invisible shoulders." Nicely rounded breast and back.

-tail: in one line with the back; closed and straight.
-position: proud and erect.
-length: 17-20 cm.; no larger, no smaller.
-plumage: short, closed, and tight. Well closed wings.
-color: as pure as possible, preferably one color, although pied is permissible.
-condition: a generally healthy impression; lively nature.

Scale of Points (Yorkshire Canary Club):

Head (20 points): Full, round, and cleanly defined. Backskull deep and carried back in line with rise of shoulders. Eye as near center of head as possible. Shoulders proportionately broad, rounded, and carried well up to and gradually merging into the head. Breast full and deep, corresponding to width and rise of shoulders and carried up full to base of beak, which should be neat and fine.

Body (10 points): Well rounded and gradually tapering throughout to tail.

Position (25 points): Attitude erect with fearless carriage, legs long without being stilty, and slight lift behind.

Feathers (25 points): Close, short, and tight. Wings proportionately long and evenly carried down the center of the back and firmly set on a compact and closely folded tail.

Size (10 points): Length approximately 16.5 cm., with corresponding symmetrical proportions.

Condition (10 points): Health, cleanliness and sound feathers, color pure and level.

Total—100 points.

CRESTED CANARY

It is possible that around 1800 the first crested Mechelse Waterslagers made their appearance. We are more certain of the crested Harz and Sakser varieties of that time. The origin of the crest is equally mysterious, although since the canary belongs to the same group of birds as the finches, the tendency toward a crest is not altogether unexpected.

Left: Lutino, characterized by total lack of pigment coupled with the presence of yellow rich coloration. **Right:** Deep Golden Green showing very good coloring but a number of defects in form.

Left: Light Yellow Isabel Melanin Pastel; the pigmentation is recognizable only as delicate diffuse cream coloration. **Right:** Golden Agate Melanin Pastel; the brownish effect is recognizable in the bird.

Thanks to mutations and of course very strict selection, the crest was developed and enlarged, probably as already mentioned, with the use of the Mechelse Waterslager. First came the crested Lancashire and later the crested Norwich. In order to improve upon the crest, the two birds were cross-bred. Lancashire x Norwich produced an intermediate crested bird which was called the crested canary. Currently, crested canaries come both without and with a crest, although unfortunately they are quite scarce. For further breeding a pairing of these two types is strongly recommended. The crested canary was developed by Mr. F.W. Barnett from Falkenham, Norfolk (1880).

Characteristics:
- crest: as large as possible, consisting of broad feathers that form a well radiating circular crest, the center of which is preferably in the center of the head. Crest should be as flat as possible, but without interruption, even on the neck. Dark crests are preferred.
- beak: fine and narrow.
- neck: well filled.
- body: looks like that of a goldfinch, with full breast and broad back. Closed feathering; flank feathers can measure up to 6 cm.
- legs: short and smooth.
- tail: short and slender.
- wings: the tips may not fall over the rump; they should be touching but not overlapping.
- position: the imaginary line we wish our bird to parallel would be at an angle of 45°.
- color: one color, preferably with melanin-colored crest.
- condition: healthy and lively.

We would like to emphasize here again that crest x crest will produce the lethal factor (25%). We therefore recommend crest x crest-bred.

For the first few days the young chicks should be fed egg food, but as soon as their beaks are strong enough they should be weaned to rape seed.

Scale of Points:
Crest (to 45 points)
Beak (5 points)
Neck (5 points)
Body (10 points)
Feet (5 points)
Plumage (10 points)
Position (10 points)
Condition (10 points)
Total—100 points
Crest-bred to 55 points.

SCOTCH FANCY

The origin of this variety is anyone's guess. We know from its name that the ancestry is Scottish; it was originally known as the "Glasgow Fancy" and "Glasgow Don." In any event, it seems likely that the Belgian Bult has played some part in the development of the Scotch Fancy, although the typical hooked form has disappeared and has taken on a more bent posture. The other partner that was used to arrive at this posture variety will probably always remain a mystery. There have been some "educated guesses" made, such as the Southern Dutch Frill, but the Scotch Fancy has a definite "hump" which it inherited from the Bossu; I find it rather doubtful that the Southern Dutch Frill would have already been known in Scotland during those years. As you can see, there are still plenty of questions.

Characteristics:
- form: shape of a half moon, with high shoulders without giving a "saddle" impression.
- head and neck: fine and narrow; the neck should be thin and long, but gradually becoming thicker and fuller at the shoulders.

- shoulders: round and narrow but well proportioned.
- back: round and long, but well filled.
- tail: long, small, and fine, with the point sticking out at an angle under the perch.
- position: the bird should be standing high on its legs, with toes steadily grasping the perch. The body itself is in a semicircular posture. The bird is very active, however, and will not stand still easily.
- length: 16-17 cm., preferably larger.
- condition: as healthy and pure as possible, without any damaged feathers or legs.

Scale of Points:
Form (20 points)
Length (10 points)
Head and neck (10 points)
Shoulders and back (20 points)
Position and behavior (25 points)
Tail (5 points)
Condition (10 points)
Total—100 points

We need to watch out that the hooked form is not too exaggerated, causing a too great similarity with the Belgian Bult. The head and neck should not be too hard.

NORWICH CANARY

The birth place of the Norwich is very likely in Flanders. These birds would have arrived in Norwich by way of Belgium, and it is in Norwich that they were improved. This is based on existing illustrations in which there is a surprising likeness to the Waterslager. In any event, it is a very old race which was even considered a color canary variety for a considerable period of time. If we pursue this train of thought for a moment, then the Lizard canary will no doubt have played a role here. In any event, the Lizard was definitely cross-bred as evidenced by the silky and shiny feathers of the Norwich canary. Around 1800 the Norwich underwent several changes, again as evidenced by illustrations, so it is a fairly safe assumption that the original race dates back quite a way, probably to the eighteenth century.

In 1890 a large exhibition was held in the town of Norwich in honor of this bird, with supposedly about 400 participants! In any case, it was at this event that the standard was established for this bird, along with the scale of points for form and position. The color was no longer considered to be the big factor, and the Norwich was no longer a color canary! The big success in both England and abroad, with interruptions only during both World Wars, has been the cause of the development of a separate race (crest and crestbred) with the establishment of their own standard. At first these birds were none too popular, some having irregularly placed small groups of feathers, which caused breeders to concentrate more on properly developing the crest, in which they succeeded.

Characteristics:
- form: short beak, broad head, round, well filled, short body, and a well filled neck as well as well filled and broad breast.
- posture: the head, neck, body, and tail should follow a smooth line which parallels a 45° angle. The legs are short.
- length: 16-17 cm., preferably 16 cm.
- wings: well closed and short; the tips should be touching and cover the root of the tail.
- feathering: silky and close.
- tail: closed, short, and held straight.
- condition: healthy and relaxed in movement.

Scale of Points (Southern Norwich Plainhead Canary Club):

Type (25 points): Short and cobby. Back broad and well filled in, showing a slight rise transversely. Chest broad and deep, giving an expansive curved front, and sweeping under from there in one full curve to the tail. Ideal length 6 to 6¼ inches. Stance or position at about an angle of 45°.

Head (10 points): Proportionately bold and assertive in its carriage. A full forehead rising from a short neat beak. To be well-rounded over and across the skull. Cheeks full and clean-featured, eye to be well placed and unobscured.

Neck (10 points): Short and thick, continuing to run from the back skull on to the shoulders, and from a full throat into the breast.

Wings (10 points): Short and well braced, meeting nicely at the tips to rest lightly, yet closely, on the rump.

Tail (5 points): Short, closely packed, and well filled in at the root. Rigidly carried, giving an all-of-one-piece appearance with the body.

Legs and feet (5 points): Well set back. Feet perfect.

Condition (10 points): In full bloom of perfect health. Bold and bouncing movement.

Quality of feather (10 points): Close and fine in texture, presenting the smooth silky plumage necessary to give a clean-cut contour.

Color (10 points): Rich, bright, and level throughout, with sheen or brilliancy. Yellows a deep orange. Buffs rich in ground color and well mealed.

Staging (5 points): Clean and correctly staged.

Total—100 points.

The little groups of feathers which are located on the head and form a crest (in so-called "lumps") can be the result of too much crossing of frosted x frosted.

BORDER CANARY

Judging from the name, we can assume that this canary

originated along the border of England and Scotland. Since both the Scots and the English claimed the honor of developing this bird, it was given the name of Border Canary to keep everyone happy! This took place in 1891.

The Border canary was originally only 13 cm. in length and was called the "wee gem" because of its size. Through the years the size increased to 15 cm. The standard established in 1930 came about through a drawing of the "ideal Border canary" made by N. Norman. The well-known German artist H. Heinzel made a new drawing in 1968 which carefully took in details regarding size, form, posture, etc.

Characteristics:
- position: erect, relaxed, with wings laying flat and closed.
- length: 14-15 cm.
- plumage: close, silky, and smooth.
- form: nicely rounded head, straight line from back to tail; somewhat rounded throat; flowing roundness from breast to stomach.
- wings: well closed.
- legs and feet: medium length; only a small part of the thighs should be visible.
- tail: tail feathers should be fairly close together; tail should be slender.
- color: soft but varied.
- condition: healthy and lively, without faults.

Scale of Points (Border Fancy Canary Club):

Head (10 points): Small, round, and neat-looking; beak fine; eyes central to roundness of head and body.

Body (15 points): Back well filled and nicely rounded, running in almost a straight line from a gentle rise over the shoulders to the point of the tail. Chest also nicely rounded, but neither heavy nor prominent, the line gradually tapering to the vent.

Wings (10 points): Compact and carried close to the body, just meeting at tips, a little lower than the root of the tail.

Legs (5 points): Of medium length, showing little thigh, fine and in harmony with the other points, yet corresponding.

Plumage (10 points): Close, firm, fine in quality, presenting a smooth, glossy, silken appearance, free from frill or roughness.

Tail (5 points): Close-packed and narrow, being nicely rounded and filled in at the root.

Position (15 points): Semi-erect, standing at an angle of 60°.

Carriage: Gay, jaunty, with full poise of the head.

Color (15 points): Rich, soft, and pure, as level in tint as possible throughout, but extreme depth and hardness such as color feeding gives are debarred.

Health (10 points): Condition and cleanliness shall have due weight.

Size (5 points): Not to exceed 5½ inches in length.

Total—100 points.

GLOSTER CORONA

A very recent addition to the family of posture canaries is the Gloster, which was bred by Mrs. Rogerson from Cheltenham in 1925. This little canary can also be thankful for its popularity to Mr. J. McLey, a Scotch show judge. The Gloster came about through a cross between the Norwich and the small Border, the progeny of which were selected for their "small size" factor and bred together. Through constant careful selection, Mrs. Rogerson was able to show this little miniature under the posture canary group in the Crystal Palace in London in 1925.

There are two types: the Gloster Corona with a crest or crown, and the uncrested Gloster Consort. Both bird varieties need to be used in breeding, because crest x crest produces a 25% lethal factor.

Characteristics:
- Corona (crest): round and symmetrical with the center point coinciding with the center point of the head. Crown should have no interruptions and radiate evenly; must not cover the eyes.
- Consort (uncrested): head should not be too small; reveal light brows.
- legs and feet: medium in length.
- body: well rounded and filled, but somewhat short and stocky.
- length: to about 11½ cm. is seen as the ideal length.
- position: active and lively, semi-erect and proud.
- plumage: smooth and well closed.
- condition: lively, healthy, and smooth feathering.

Scale of Points (Gloster Fancy Canary Club):

Corona (15 points): Neatness, regular, unbroken round shape, eye discernible. (5 points): With definite center.

Consort (15 points): Head broad and round at every point, with good rise over center of skull. (5 points): Eyebrow heavy, showing brow.

Body (20 points): Back well filled and wings lying closely thereto; full neck; chest nicely rounded, without prominence.

Tail (5 points): Closely folded and well carried.

Plumage (15 points): Close, firm, giving a clear-cut appearance; of good natural color.

Carriage (10 points): Alert, with quick lively movement.

Legs and feet (5 points): Medium length, without blemish.

Size (15 points): For tendency to the diminutive.

Condition (10 points): Health, cleanliness.

Total—100 points.

LIZARD CANARY

Toward the end of the sixteenth century, the Huguenots fled to England and brought their pets along with them, among which was their type of canary. The Lizard completed its development in England, although this race, which is undoubtedly one of the oldest posture races that we know today, did not undergo many changes in its first four hundred years. This race had once been very popular, but after the Second World War an article in the English bird magazine *Cage Birds* requesting cooperation in compiling a census of these birds came up with a mere thirty couples. Through a very active breeding program the number of Lizards has been greatly increased, so that currently these lovely birds are quite common. Their so-called "spangles" set them apart from other canaries and remind us a lot of the scales of a lizard, which is obviously how they got their name. Every canary breeder will know that this marking effect is due to the fact that the tips of the feathers are colorless and will only gain color after the juvenile molt. Somewhat older canaries will get broader feather edges, which of course will cost them the markings on the back; this unfortunate step backward in attractiveness can also be observed in their wings and tail, which should be black, as should the beak, legs, and feet. Nowadays there are also agate brown and isabel Lizards. In addition, it is interesting to note that there are also some secondary colors, such as the non-intensive yellow with the ordinary Lizard, the intensive golden yellow with the gold Lizard, the white with the blue Lizard, and the red factor with the bronze Lizard. It is altogether possible that we will soon be able to inbreed the non-classical lipochrome and melanin colors.

From all of this we can conclude that the Lizard may well be a color and color marking canary, and this kind of idea is common enough. However, according to the C.O.M. it is at least partially a posture canary, and this was maintained

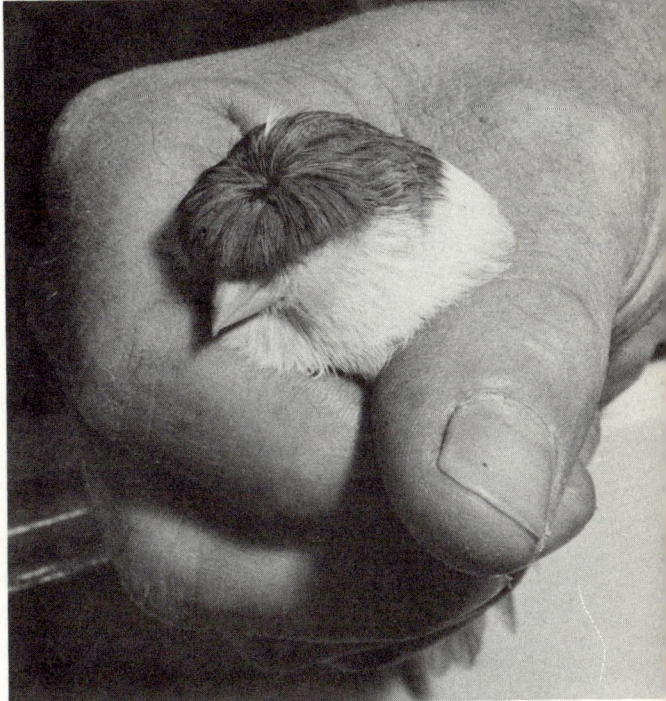

A very good Corona, with a good center and a good drop. The experienced exhibitor would gently remove the small white feather with a tweezer.

at the congress in Munich in 1972, and seeing the characteristic breast, the position and the size of the Lizard, this certainly seems to be a valid standpoint.

Characteristics:
- ground color: yellow-white or red factor.
- cap: same as ground color, so yellow-white or red factor.
- spangles: the "scale" markings can be black, agate, brown, or isabel; the same applies to the rowings, the marking on the underside of the body.
- type of coloring: intensive or frosted.
- back markings: should be regular and even, starting at the neck and becoming larger on the back.
- plumage: smooth and well closed, giving a silky impression.

Scale of Points:
Spangles (25 points): For regularity and distinctness.
Feather quality (15 points): For tightness and silkiness.
Ground color (10 points): For depth and evenness.
Breast (10 points): For extent and regularity of rowings.
Wings and tail (10 points): For neatness and darkness.
Cap (10 points): For neatness and shape.
Covert feathers (5 points): For darkness and lacing.
Eyelash (5 points): For regularity and clarity.
Beak, legs, and feet (5 points): For darkness.
Steadiness and staging (5 points).
Total—100 points.

PARISIAN FRILL

In this variety there lurk some real giants of the canary world, some of which have tail feathers that alone measure 12 cm.! It would seem obvious that they have not always been this large (I saw some birds in Brazil that exceeded 22 cm.!), but we know very little about the origin of this race, though many experts think that the Northern Dutch Frill should be considered the forefather. The Parisian Frill completed its development in Paris and surrounding areas, and in 1867 an organization already existed honoring this variety. This lovely bird is certainly deserving of the attention, with its robust build, the proud posture, and the symmetry of its tightly curled frills. The better these three points, the higher a score a Parisian Frill will be able to claim at a show.

Characteristics:
- length: 19-22 cm.; circumference of the feathering: 28-30 cm.
- position: semi-erect, proud and brave.
- plumage: evenly distributed frills, which should be fine.

- mantle: abundant and well developed shoulder and back frills.
- breast: well filled with symmetrical breast frills.
- flanks: symmetrical with mantle and breast feathers.
- tail frills: these are located at the root of the tail, should be olive-shaped, and look something like rooster feathers. They should be long and full and fall evenly from the rump.
- head and neck feathers: there are two possibilities here: either "casquette" type where the curled feathers form a perfect transition to the smooth head, or "calotte" type where the feathers make a curly transition to a frilled head.
- legs and feet: should be well developed; the toe nails may grow in the shape of a corkscrew.
- tail: closed, long and broad; a swallow's tail or indented bottom edge is considered a serious fault.
- wings: well closed and long.
- condition: healthy, proud, and very clean.

Scale of Points (C.O.M.)

Size and shape (10 points): From 19 to 22 cm. Well built.

Feathering: (10 points): Very even. Fine and long or crisp and short.

Position (10 points): Well poised. Massive and symmetrical disposition of feathers.

Mantle (15 points): Abundant and well developed, with frills reaching almost to the rump.

Breast feathers (10 points): Double frills, well furnished and symmetrical.

Flanks (10 points): Symmetrical with mantle and jabot. Rising well over the wings and shoulders.

Head and neck (8 points): Frills on the head of the "calotte" or "casquette" type. Perfect transition from head to body.

Tail coverts (5 points): Falling evenly from the rump on either side.

Wings (5 points): Long and close to the body.

Legs and feet (5 points): Well developed. Nails like a corkscrew.

Tail (4 points): Long and large. Ends of the quills in line.

Condition (8 points): Vigorous, with poise. General impression massive and symmetrical.

Total—100 points.

GIBBER ITALICUS OR ITALIAN HUMPBACK FRILL

The Gibber, as it is known on the Continent, looks identical in shape to the Southern Dutch Frill and belongs to the Frilled Posture Canary group. The Southern Dutch Frill will, no doubt, have played a role in the development of the form of the Gibber, which is, however, a smaller bird, but it has maintained the nervous nature of the Southern Dutch Frill.

It may sound a little strange, but the Italian Humpback Frill is really the end result of erroneous breeding. Continuous breeding of intensive birds caused the feathers to become more and more sparse, to the point where the breast and thighs ended up bald. The small size can also be blamed on the intensive factor. But it is just this nakedness of the thighs and breast that makes a good Gibber Italicus! It stands to reason that only experienced breeders have success in breeding this somewhat strange looking canary, because a certain insight and intuition is required to enable a breeder to know just how far the intensive x intensive can be bred. Many young die before or just after coming out of the egg or when they are still very young.

Characteristics:
- head and neck: "snaky," small head and beak. The neck is

carried in a horizontal position. Both head and neck should be smoothly feathered.
- shoulders: high, with symmetrical frills.
- body: rounded, semi-erect.
- tail: narrow and pointed straight down, preferably close to the perch, but not against it or under it.
- position: generally following a figure 7.
- legs: long and stiff, stretched out.
- plumage: sparse, with some frills on shoulders, flanks, and breast; thighs and breast are naked.
- length: 16-17 cm., preferably smaller.

Scale of Points (C.O.M.):
Position (20 points): In the form of a figure 7.
Head (6 points): Small and fine, narrow skull, small back, no frills.
Neck (15 points): Long and horizontal, no frills.
Legs (15 points): Long and stiff, thighs exposed.
Wings (6 points): Long and close to the body.
Shoulders (10 points); High, with symmetrical frills.
Tail (6 points): Long, vertical, pressed to the perch.
Breast (10 points): Breastbone naked, frills not meeting in the center.
Flanks (6 points): Symmetrical on both sides, holding the wings.
Length (6 points): 16-17 cm. preferably smaller.
Total—100 points.

NORTHERN DUTCH FRILL

If we gave the impression that the previous variety hailed from the Netherlands, we will have to say that this is not a certainty by any means; in fact, the origin of the Northern Dutch Frill is also rather obscure. We would add, though, that according to the experts there is a definite possibility that the first frilled canaries came from the Netherlands. If we delve into this matter from the point of view of language, the birth place could well be the northern part of Paris, since the Northern Dutch Frill is known as the "Noordhollandse frise," with Hollandse possibly meaning the likeness to the Dutch national costume of that time.

Legendre, an old member of the Comite Ornithologique International, says the following on the topic: "The Dutch laid the foundation for the frilled canaries. Their first interests were concentrated on the area of selecting long feathered canaries. Through these long feathers, which originally were concentrated mostly on the breast and soon started to fall somewhat open, a comparison to Dutch national dress was obvious. From the drawings we were given to examine, the feathering on the back and flanks also became thicker, not so much in the form of curls but more like a scoop. The breeding of

The robustly built Parisian Frill and a pied canary can enjoy a ready supply of energy from the sugar in the fruit.

this variety spread to Belgium and then to the northern areas of France, especially in Roubaix and even further south to Picardie, where the Frill was named 'Roubaisien' and 'Picardien.' Later he was named the Northern Dutch Frill. If we delve further into the history of this frilled variety, we will see that the breeding of this bird went as far south as Paris, where the Parisian Frill was then developed."

Characteristics:
- head and neck: small and without frills; slightly raised.
- mantle: without many curled feathers; symmetrical.
- breast feathering: fairly well developed; symmetrical.
- flanks: curled feathers directed upwards; symmetrical.
- legs: fairly long and slightly bent; thighs should be well covered by feathers.
- length: 17 cm.
- position: proud and erect.
- condition: lively, healthy and clean.

Scale of Points (C.O.M.)

Legs and feet (10 points): Long thighs, normally feathered, legs not too bent.

Head and neck (15 points): Small and without frills, slightly raised.

Size (10 points): About 17 cm.

Mantle (15 points): Symmetrical, well proportioned, without any additional frilling.

Flanks (15 points): Full, bulky, even, rising toward the shoulders.

Breast (15 points): Frills symmetrical and complete.

Condition (10 points): Healthy, clean, and entire.

Plumage (10 points): Frills undamaged and symmetrical.

Total—100 points.

SOUTHERN DUTCH FRILL

Although the name would not give it away, this frill really originated in Italy, specifically from around Naples, Vaserte, Benevente, and southern Italy. This variety probably inherited the high back from the Belgian Bult and the frills from the Northern Dutch Frill. It is also presumed that the Southern Dutch Frill contributed to the development of the Gibber Italicus. As far as can be determined the Southern Dutch Frill first appeared after the First World War and about twenty years later reached its peak. The bird was fairly well proportioned, the shape of a figure 7 was practically perfected, and the shape of the head was much like that of a lizard. When the bird sits on the perch, his legs are stretched out and the tail almost touches the perch. A characteristic of this variety is that they are very nervous, which can be seen during exhibitions, with the bird moving from side to side and regularly holding onto the front of the cage with one foot. This is why the scale of points allows for such behavior, since it is so typical. It is unfortunate that this bird has become quite rare and the breeding material which is still available is rather heavily inbred, so degeneration is anything but imaginary. If there were some good breeding material available, this interesting frill would certainly be able to capture more fans.

Characteristics:
- head and neck: small head, like a lizard; small beak. Neck is elongated and "snaky" in appearance.
- position: ideally a figure 7. Head and neck should stick out. The wings should be somewhat erect. Tail bends inward a little, almost touching the perch. Thighs should be well covered with feathering. Feet are stretched out.
- body: well rounded and long.
- length: 16-17 cm.

- mantle: symmetrical frills; regular and full.
- breast feathers: curling toward each other from left to right, and symmetrical (jabots). The frills give the impression that they form a little basket.
- flanks: these feathers should curl upward and be equally long on both flanks; also symmetrical and full.
- tail: long and especially well closed; as mentioned, slightly bent inward, almost touching the tail.
- wings: well closed, but the tips must not overlap.
- plumage: undamaged and soft.
- condition: brisk, proud, and healthy.

Scale of Points:
　Position and form (20 points)
　Length (10 points)
　Head (10 points)
　Neck (10 points)
　Mantle (10 points)
　Breast feathers (10 points)
　Flanks (10 points)
　Legs and feet (10 points)
　Tail (10 points)
　Total—100 points

BERNESE CANARY

This posture canary is the national Swiss canary. Although carrying the name of Switzerland's capital, it was not necessarily developed there, as a canary often inherits the name of an area or town, such as the Norwich and Yorkshire canaries. When we go back into the history of canary breeding, we will see that the Swiss have long occupied themselves with the developing of a canary race of their own. There is also a Swiss Frill, which was officially recognized in 1967 in Germany and in 1968 in France, though they are still quite rare. Every somewhat different mutation, however, was not just approved and developed into a special type. No, the Swiss wanted a race that would stand out for its proud posture and slender form, and it was to be as pure as the Swiss Alps themselves. This finally became the Bernese canary, a bird that stands very tall and erect and is still somewhat stocky but nevertheless makes an attractive impression.

It is likely that this bird was bred in the beginning of the twentieth century, because in 1910 a great many breeders already knew of it. It was around this time that a standard drawing and a scale of points were established. Various crosses, back-crosses, and selection have been necessary to perfect the Bernese canary. In this connection it is interesting (though a little strange) that a Bernese canary came into the spotlight in an exhibition in Lisbon in 1966, where Mr. R. Koch participated with a series of Bernese canaries that surprised everyone. They were of a very high quality. A renewed introduction, this one on an international basis, has been the cause of the Bernese canary now having enthusiasts in many different countries.

Characteristics:
- position: well proportioned, elegant, and reasonably corpulent. The posture should be very erect and proud.
- length: 16-17 cm.
- head: short and broad with a short, flattened skull.
- neck: quite long and thick.
- breast: well developed and massive.
- wings: long and closed; tips should not overlap.
- shoulders: sturdy and well marked.
- tail: long, narrow, and forming one line with the back.
- legs: long, with a slight bend at the heels.
- plumage: full, smooth, and fine.
- color: one color or variegated; must be quite shiny.

A Norwich Crestbred. It may be found occasionally that Norwich hens are not always the best mothers (which may be said of hens of other breeds as well) but this is rarely so if the big, heavy type of bird is avoided. By nature such birds are sometimes rather clumsy and inactive, whereas the medium-sized, smarter type of hen is as a rule much more lively and energetic in attending to her duties.

Scale of Points:
  Position (20 points)
  Head (20 points)
  Neck (15 points)
  Wings (15 points)
  Legs (10 points)
  Plumage (10 points)
  General Appearance (10 points)
  Total—100 points

FINAL NOTES

There are yet some other posture canaries, but they are quite rare, so it does not seem worthwhile to include them. I would like, however, to make a few more notes regarding the judging of show birds.

A Buff Norwich canary. The official standard says that the type has to be: "Short and cobby. Back broad and well filled in, showing a slight rise transversely. Chest broad and deep, giving an expansive curved front, and sweeping under therefrom in one full curve to the tail. Ideal length 6 to 6¼ inches. Stance or position at about an angle of 45 degrees."

If any canary is dependent upon judging, it is definitely the posture canary. This does have the inherent danger that canaries can become the "victims" of the experimental goals of their keepers. I will not even touch on the many crosses that are brought about in an attempt to arrive at deviating shapes, and I also prefer to remain silent about these breeders who, from a commercial point of view, simply breed their birds at random, discarding any requirements and standards that have been set forth by the various bird clubs and associations. It is the business and concern of breeders to be aware of the requirements and standards of posture canaries. A little knowledge is sometimes just as bad as none at all, with breeders attempting to correct mistakes that are not mistakes at all, and the other way around by introducing characteristics that are not actually desirable!

A well-known example of this was the introduction of Norwich blood into the Border canary to give it a "heavier" look. This is something that should definitely not take place. The Border, after all, is a small posture canary. In addition, such a cross brings with it black brows and the filled neck, also not desirable traits for the Border. The Gloster, as another example, is all too often muddled with the crossing of ordinary color canaries. If we want to maintain good posture canaries, we will have to avoid such practices.

Consequently, it is the show judges' job to be very selective and strict and to punish any less than top quality birds with low scores. In conclusion, I would like to list here the C.O.M. key for posture canaries.

Category A: Frilled Canaries
1. Parisian Frilled Canary
    a. Color frill
    b. Badouaner

2. Northern Dutch Frill
3. Southern Dutch Frill
   one-colored
4. Swiss Frill
5. Gibber Italicus

Category B: Posture Canaries
1. Belgian Bult
2. Scotch Fancy
3. Munchner (not recognized by C.O.M.)
4. Japanese Hoso (not recognized by C.O.M.)

Category C: Form Canaries
1. Border Fancy
2. Raza Espagnola
3. Norwich
4. Yorkshire
   a. Continental type
   b. English type
5. Bernese Canary

Category D: Crested Canaries
1. Gloster
   a. Corona
   b. Consort
2. German
   a. crested
   b. non-crested
3. Crested Canary
   a. crested
   b. crest-bred
4. Lancashire
   a. crested
   b. non-crested

The Norwich Crest. Today five different specialist societies cater to the needs of the Norwich canary. In spite of the turbulent episodes in its past history, the Norwich remains a breed of great merit and distinction.

Category E: Marked Canaries
1. Lizard
    a. Silver
    b. Yellow
    c. Red
    d. Clear-capped
    e. Broken-capped
    f. Non-capped

Bibliography

Arnall, L. and I.F. Keymer, *Bird diseases.* Neptune, 1975.
Bates, H. and R. Busenbark, *Finches and soft-billed birds.** Neptune, 1970.
Boosey, Edward J., *Foreign bird keeping.* London.
Dodwell, G.T., *Canaries.* Edinburgh.
Dost, Helmuth, *Handbuch der Vogelpfege und-zuchtung.* Leipzig, 1954.
Evans, I., *All about canaries.** Neptune, 1976.
Legendre, Marcel, *Oiseaux de cage.* Paris, 1952.
Low, R., *Beginner's guide to birdkeeping.* London, 1974.
Lynch, G., *Canaries in colour.* Poole, 1976.
Lynch, G., *Canaries, their care and breeding.* Leicester.
Naether, Carl and M.M. Vriends, *Building an aviary.** Neptune, 1978.
Newby, Cliff, *Canaries for pleasure and profit.** Neptune.
Risdon, D.H.S., *Foreign birds for beginners.* London, 1953.
Rogers, C.H., *Encyclopaedia of cage and aviary birds.* New York and London, 1975.
Rutgers, A., *Encyclopedia of aviculture.* Vol. III. Poole, 1977.
Rutgers, A., *The handbook of foreign birds,* Vol. I and II. Poole, 1977.
Smet, G., *Canaris couleurs. Le Canari du Harz.* Les Coudreau. Chelles, 1947.
Smet, G., *Les canaris.* Paris, 1953.
Speicher, Klaus, *Canary varieties.** Neptune, 1979.

Stork, C.J., *Kanaries*. Amsterdam, 1979.
Stroud, R., *Diseases of canaries.* * Neptune.
Veerkamp, H.J., *Handleiding voor de kleurkanariekweker*. Zutphen, 1967.
Vriends, Th., *ABC voor de vogelliefhebber*. Baarn, 1979.
Vriends, Th., *Mijn eerste voliere*. Den Haag, 1979.
Vriends, Th., *Prisma kanarieboek*. Utrecht, 1979.
Vriends, M., *Starting an aviary.* * Neptune, 1980.
Walker, G.B.R.., *Coloured canaries*. Poole, 1976.

*Titles marked with an asterisk are published by T.F.H. Publications, Inc. and are available at pet shops and bird specialty stores everywhere.

ILLUSTRATIONS INDEX

A
Agate, 300 (Deep Red-Melanin Pastel), 305 (Light Red), 305 (Deep Bronze-Opal), 308 (Red-Lipochrome Melanin Pastel), 308 (Light Green-Melanin Pastel), 312 (Deep Red-Lipochrome Pastel), 313 (Silver), 316 (Silver), 320 Golden-Melanin Pastel)
Aviaries, 38, 63, 64, 67, 71, 75, 79

B
Bathing, 175, 190, 206
Belgian Bult, 300
Birdroom, See Cages; Aviaries
Bird Show, 249, 265
Border, Frontis (Green), 6 (Hen with Young), 12 (Male), 100, 217 (Hen with Young), 247
Border Fancy, 13 (Green), 16, 19, 20 (Green), 30 (Green), 32, 34 (Hen), 35, 65 (Clear Yellow), 76, 81 (Young), 84, 88 (Young), 91 (Cock), 94 (Hen), 96 (Hen), 116 (Young), 118 (Variegated Hen with Young), 126 (Young), 135 (Hen with Young), 136, 138, 140 (Cock with Young), 143, 145 (Variegated), 154 (Cock and Female), 156 (Adults and Young), 157, 162, 163, 165, 168, 169, 171 (Young), 179 (Cock), 216 (Young), 231, 234 (Cinnamon), 235 (Cinnamon), 242, 243, 245, 250 (Cinnamon), 261
Bronze, 304 (Deep)
Brown, 304 (Light Yellow), 308 (Deep Golden)
Bullfinch, 267
Cages, 36, 39, 40 (Commercial), 41 (Show), 42 (Show), 43 (Commercial), 45 (Show), 46 (Breeding), 48 (Breeding), 50, 51, 57, 58 (Breeding), 60, 62, 65, 75, 251 (Breeding), 265 (Show)
Chicks, 131, 133, 142, 279 (with Hen), 287
"Commercial" Canary, 236, 285
Crested, 69, 204, 211 (Grizzled), 288

D
Dutch Frill, 293

E
Eggs, 129, 207

F
Fawn Piebald-spotted, 293
Fawn Slate, 293
Feather Structure, 151, 152
Feeding, 83, 322, 336
Feeding Stand, 79
Frills, English Type, 120, 256
Frills, Parisian, 26, 293, 309, 312, 336

G
Gibber Italicus, 317
Gloster Fancy, 16, 19, 27, 86 (Young), 99 (Cock), 196, 216, 227 (Green Hen with Young), 233 (Young), 273, 297, 313 (Consort)
Gloster Fancy Corona, 27, 99 (Cock), 164, 167 (Crested, 170, 238 (Crested), 301 (Buff), 316, 331
Green, 73, 300 (Light), 320 (Deep Golden)

H
Handfeeding, 199, 237
Hooded Siskin, 8

I
Illness, 180, 184, 188
Isabel, 304 (Deep Golden-Melanin Pastel), 309 (Silver Opal), 312 (Red), 317 (Red Mosaic Hen), 317 (Light Red), 317 (Dark Red), 320 (Light Yellow-Melanin Pastel)
Italian Humpback Frill, See Gibber Italicus

L
Lancashire Coppy, 10, 197, 259, 262, 266
Lipochrome Pastel, 305 (Light Red Opal), 308 (Light Red and Black), 309 (Deep Red and Black), 312 (Deep Red Agate)
Lizard Canary, 11, 77, 111, 176, 214 (Breeding), 301 (Blue), 301 (Golden), 309 (Red)
Lutino, 320

M
Melanin Pastel, 300 (Deep Red Agate), 304 (Deep Golden Isabel), 305 (Light Red Brown), 308 (Red Agate Lipochrome), 308 (Light Green Agate), 320 (Light Yellow Isabel), 320 (Golden Agate)

N
Nail Clipping, 188, 194
Nest, 80 (with Chicks)
Nest Pan, 54, 72, 108, 186
New Color Canary, 212, 213, 289, 292
North Hollander, 300
Norwich, 24, 28, 58, 102, 124 (Young), 160, 173, 180 (with "Lumps"), 193, 226, 235 (Cock), 239, 267, 275, 301 (Buff), 341 (Crestbred), 342 (Buff), 345 (Crest)

P
Phaeo-Ino, 296, 313 (Silver Brown)
Pied, 336

R
Red, 316 (Light)
Red and Black, 304 (Light)
Red Factor Canary, 200 (Hen), 201 (Cock), 220, 221, 228 (Adults with Young)
Red Mosaic, 313 (Hen)
Roller, 62, 106 (Young), 112 (Hen at Nest), 115 (Young)

S
Scotch Fancy, 68, 255

Sooty-Black, 209
Supplies, 53, 137

T
Taming, 270, 272

W
Whites, 240 (Show Hen)

Y
Yellow, 21, 22 (Pigmented), 284, 312 (Deep Golden)
Yorkshire, 14, 23, 85, 92, 93, 104, 148, 177, 205, 208, 224, 253 (Hen), 274, 316